Getting the Message Across

Using Slideware Effectively in Technical Presentations

Stéphane Faroult

Apress®

Getting the Message Across: Using Slideware Effectively in Technical Presentations

Stéphane Faroult

ISBN-13 (pbk): 978-1-4842-2294-2   ISBN-13 (electronic): 978-1-4842-2295-9
DOI 10.1007/978-1-4842-2295-9

Library of Congress Control Number: 2016959515

Managing Director: Welmoed Spahr
Lead Editor: Jonathan Gennick
Development Editor: Laura Berendson
Editorial Board: Steve Anglin, Pramila Balan, Laura Berendson, Aaron Black, Louise Corrigan,
    Jonathan Gennick, Todd Green, Robert Hutchinson, Celestin Suresh John, Nikhil Karkal,
    James Markham, Susan McDermott, Matthew Moodie, Natalie Pao, Gwenan Spearing
Coordinating Editor: Jill Balzano
Copy Editor: Karen Jameson
Compositor: SPi Global
Indexer: SPi Global
Cover Designer: eStudio Calamar

Distributed to the book trade worldwide by Springer Science+Business Media New York, 233 Spring Street, 6th Floor, New York, NY 10013. Phone 1-800-SPRINGER, fax (201) 348-4505, e-mail orders-ny@springer-sbm.com, or visit www.springer.com. Apress Media, LLC is a California LLC and the sole member (owner) is Springer Science + Business Media Finance Inc (SSBM Finance Inc). SSBM Finance Inc is a **Delaware** corporation.

For information on translations, please e-mail rights@apress.com, or visit www.apress.com.

Apress and friends of ED books may be purchased in bulk for academic, corporate, or promotional use. eBook versions and licenses are also available for most titles. For more information, reference our Special Bulk Sales–eBook Licensing web page at www.apress.com/bulk-sales.

Any source code or other supplementary materials referenced by the author in this text are available to readers at www.apress.com. For detailed information about how to locate your book's source code, go to www.apress.com/source-code/. Readers can also access source code at SpringerLink in the Supplementary Material section for each chapter.

Printed on acid-free paper

Contents at a Glance

Contents

About the Author

Stéphane Faroult is known as a database consultant and author. He is also at times a college instructor. He has spent a good deal of his consultancy career not only fixing problems but also explaining to groups of people why the problem occurred in the first place, which led to creating courses and seminars that he gave both in his native French and in English. The necessity of explaining system architectures and potential traps that were hard to replicate and demonstrate, as well as in another context to students what was really happening inside a computer, led him to use what is generically known as "slideware" in a very visual way – to transfer his painfully acquired own understanding as efficiently as possible.

Acknowledgments

The first person I have to thank is also my first reader, Sandra Peele, whose remarks helped me clarify the text, and occasionally led me to redesigning figures; her redoing my examples with a different version of PowerPoint from the one I had been using, which is far more than I was expecting of her, also helped me write a more generic text with a focus on principles rather than details. I must also thank Sara Whalen and those of her COMM311 students at K-State who commented on a kind of early video draft; their remarks helped me better structure this book.

Needless to say, my warm thanks go to all the people at Apress who have helped me turn my book project into the real thing: my editor Laura Berendson; as well as my old acquaintance Jonathan Gennick; and Jill Balzano, the coordinating editor with whom I already had the pleasure to work with, but as a technical reviewer instead of author. A special thanks to Karen Jameson, the Copyeditor and eStudio Calamar, the cover designer of this book.

Introduction

That's what all we are. Amateurs. We don't live long enough to be anything else.

—Charlie Chaplin (1889-1977)

Among the numerous books that exist about presentations and visual aids, the present book features a number of originalities: it focuses on technical presentations; it pleads for a quasi-cinematic use of "slides"; and it was written by someone who, so far, has never tried to make a cent designing presentations for others, or teaching others how to do it. In fact, the thousands of slides I have created were for my own usage, with the exception of a couple of cases when I have helped friends with their presentations.

I'm better known as a database specialist; in this capacity I have had to deliver tons of presentations over the years: technical sales presentations, professional training, conferences, and seminars. I have also created a number of short video tutorials on YouTube. I'm not completely foreign to teaching students either, as I taught various Computer Science courses at the University of Ottawa in the mid-1980s; and, thirty years later, in French higher-education institutes; and at Kansas State University, where I taught, full-time, four terms in the Computer Science department. I have talked on technical topics in my native French and in English, in at least eight different countries on three continents. My audience was sometimes composed of people whose native language was the language I was talking in (occasionally a different version from what I have been taught), and sometimes composed of people who probably couldn't understand me any more easily than I could understand them. Circumstances (to which you can add, in a number of cases, jet lag) that were enough to motivate me in trying to better communicate visually.

The Shoulders of Giants

Isaac Newton famously said that if he had seen further, it's because he had been standing on the shoulders of giants. Nobody has innate knowledge of presentations; I don't feel too proud of most of my early presentations, but I worked hard to improve what I was doing. I've had two epiphanies. The first one was when I stumbled by chance on a video recording of a presentation called *Identity 2.0* delivered at the OSCON conference in 2005 by a Canadian named Dick Hardt (you can easily find this presentation on the Web). It was fast, funny, and brilliant. Hardt acknowledged his debt to a famous law professor, Lawrence Lessig, whose presentation style inspired him, but his tempo was much faster and there was an undeniable personal touch. This presentation demonstrated to me firstly that you don't need to have one idea and three to five bullet points by slide as I had always read everywhere; and secondly the importance of rhythm.

The second epiphany was, out of necessity, a series of seminars I gave in Asia. When you know that you'll have to fly from Paris to Beijing to talk for two days before jumping in a plane to repeat the operation in Shanghai, Hong Kong, and Singapore before flying back home, you can suppose that it will be tough, and I wasn't disappointed. At the same time, whenever you are talking abroad, especially far away, you feel obliged to stand up to the "international expert" label that is automatically stuck upon you and to meet high expectations, even if you wake up in the middle of the night not to find sleep again. I knew before my trip that I would have to rely on a robust, visual deck of slides to save me, and I worked far harder on it than I would have done for a similar talk in Paris (and in French).

These two epiphanies triggered in me a strong interest for how to best use PowerPoint, a tool that is much derided by some people, and I began reading on the topic. I believe that one of the first books that said "you don't have to make boring presentations with PowerPoint" is a book called *Beyond Bullet Points*,[1] by Cliff Atkinson, which I haven't read but that enjoys a flattering repute. On its heels were published two other books that I have bought and read: *Presentation Zen*[2] by Garr Reynolds, and *Slide:ology*[3] by Nancy Duarte. Both books share a similar philosophy; Garr Reynolds, who teaches design at a Japanese university, focuses more on the clarity of slides, and Nancy Duarte on the story line, but there are echoes between the two books. I have a slight preference for Garr Reynolds's book, perhaps because I read it first and as a result *Slide:ology* was less of an eye-opener for me; both books are very good, and the authors' sites are useful resources (www.garrreynolds.com and www.duarte.com).

Some books not directly connected to PowerPoint have also been quite inspirational. I read a very long time ago *Ogilvy on Advertising*,[4] by David Ogilvy, and many of his principles can be directly applied to presentations. If you need to visually show numbers, I can warmly recommend a book that is considered a classic: *The Visual Display of Quantitative Information*,[5] by Edward Tufte; you will no longer look at charts in the same way after reading it. In the footsteps of Tufte, but perhaps more directly practical, one can recommend the books of Stephen Few, whose site (www.perceptualedge.com) is also rich with information.

I must quote among my sources John McWade's *How to Design Cool Stuff*,[6] a great book where I have learned much. A book that also benefited me, and which I found mentioned, to give credit where it's due, on the site of Garr Reynolds who recommends it, is a book about films, *The Visual Story*[7] by Bruce Block. I believe that a good use of PowerPoint is very movie-like, especially for technical presentations, and I have learned as much from Bruce Block as from John McWade – which is significant praise.

Finally, another small book also inspired me, *Speech-making and Presentation Made Easy*[8] by Max Atkinson (no connection with Cliff), a Briton who specializes in political speeches. What the author says about presentation aids is light; but what he says about speeches and memorable expressions is most interesting, and can in my opinion be transposed to the visual world.

I owe a huge debt to the authors of these books, and yet I wasn't quite satisfied. Some advice was very good, but somehow not quite applicable to what I had to do. It was great for product presentations, it was great for presenting strategies, it was suitable for broad-brush talks about technology delivered to a nonspecialist audience; it was not quite right for getting into the gory details, which was more my type of presentation.

Slide and Prejudice

I always find it remarkable that whenever you are putting your fingers on the image of a keyboard on the screen of a smartphone, the layout of the keys is still the one that was designed almost one century and a half ago to prevent the levers of mechanical typewriters from jamming; and I'm not sure that too many people know when they send an email that "CC" stands for "Carbon Copy." I believe that, after an interval of several

---

[1]Cliff Atkinson, *Beyond Bullet Points: Using Microsoft PowerPoint to Create Presentations That Inform, Motivate, and Inspire*, 3rd ed. (Redmond, WA: Microsoft Press, 2011).
[2]Garr Reynolds, *Presentation Zen: Simple Ideas on Presentation Design and Delivery*, 2nd ed. (Berkeley, CA: New Riders, 2011).
[3]Nancy Duarte, *Slide:ology: The Art and Science of Creating Great Presentations* (Newton, MA: O'Reilly Media, 2008).
[4]David Ogilvy, *Ogilvy on Advertising* (New York: Vintage, 1985).
[5]Edward Tufte, *The Visual Display of Quantitative Information*, 2nd ed. (Cheshire, CT: Graphics Press, 1983).
[6]John McWade, *Before and After: How to Design Cool Stuff* (Berkeley, CA: Peachpit Press, 2009).
[7]Bruce Block, *The Visual Story: Creating the Visual Structure of Film, TV and Digital Media*, 2nd ed. (New York: Focal Press, 2007).
[8]Max Atkinson, *Speech-Making and Presentation Made Easy: Seven Essential Steps to Success* (London: Vermilion, 2008).

decades, I last saw a sheet of carbon paper in use in 1991 or 1992, in a bank in Prague where I was waiting to exchange money, at a time when everything was changing very fast in (then) Czechoslovakia.

New technology tries to align itself on what it replaces. This policy facilitates adoption by users reluctant to change, but in a strange way it fossilizes old technologies when they have disappeared. The same phenomenon happened with presentation software. In the 1980s, before presentation software became popular, there were two "modern" ways of presenting: color transparencies (photographic slides), which were horribly expansive to prepare and reserved for the top brass; and overhead transparencies (sheets of transparent material), used by the rank-and-file to which I belonged. Overhead transparencies came themselves in two flavors: sheets that you had to write on with markers of various colors; and far more expensive sheets that could be used in a photocopier to obtain neat text and diagrams from a printed original - in black and white as color copiers were a rarity. You could do fun things with these transparent sheets, such as stacking them. Alignment was sometimes a bit haphazard, and after three of four sheets luminosity was decreasing dramatically; it's a technique I intensely used at the University of Ottawa to teach data structures, a staple course in any computer science curriculum.

Presentation software adopted the photographic slide paradigm, and remains stuck with it long after the disappearance of photographic slides. Almost all books on presentations, even the best ones, have for implicit axiom that the slide is the unit. It took me some time to come to challenge the axiom, and to understand that I could do with presentation software what I was doing with overhead transparencies, but far better. I slowly evolved both my style and my techniques over five years.

And then something strange happened. When I reached a decent mastery of the tool and was beginning to use it in a sophisticated way, nobody seemed to notice. I had some remarks from students or trainees about some "fun slides," but it's not difficult to create a "fun slide" – you just need a zany idea. The animations I had carefully crafted to illustrate my explanations? No remark at all. I had comments on the talk or the class as a whole (mostly positive, sometimes negative), but nothing about my slide deck in particular.

Will I say it? I was disappointed. I crave for recognition for my efforts as much as anybody else. Until I understood that for people my slides weren't a "PowerPoint presentation." I had some very positive feedback on my videos, but somebody wrote to me "I don't know which tool you are using..." What I show – plain PowerPoint – seems to appear as something else, a part of a whole, which is *my* presentation, not me commenting a set of PowerPoint slides. A friend of mine was absolutely delighted that, after a presentation I had helped her to prepare, an attendee apologized, before asking a question, for arriving when the "movie" had already started. As many of my students also seemed to understand, after some suffering, notions that have the repute to be hard to get, I came to think that, perhaps, I was doing something right. I decided to abandon my selfish ways and share what I had gathered, guessed, and experimented, within the framework of my guiding principles and, where I lack principles, my guiding prejudices. Hence this book.

Objective of This Book

Contrary to the claims of many books or tutorials, I won't try in this book to teach you how to prepare awesome slides, nor to wow your audience. I don't believe that it should be your purpose when preparing a presentation. I'll teach you how to realize sophisticated visual explanations that people seem to hardly notice but swallow, bait and hook. The purpose of any presentation is that people remember what you told them, not how great your slides were.

I don't claim that what I explain in this book is the ultimate word about how to use presentation software; I just hope that it will help readers leapfrog my years of experiments, and open new vistas to them. I've started by copying others before I have found a personal style. I'm trying in this book to give many ideas, and I hope it will trigger new ones for the most creative of my readers. I have successfully used the type of presentation I advocate in many different contexts. It seems to me to work especially well in videos.

I wrote this book thinking of anybody who has to explain to others something more down-to-earth than great ideas or general directions, which you cannot classify as "business"; anybody who has technical knowledge, of any nature, to communicate. I assume a basic knowledge of presentation software, but nothing more.

How This Book Is Structured

This book is divided into seven chapters, plus short appendices that contain material that is important but didn't really fit elsewhere.

- Chapter 1 covers general presentation design issues, layout, colors, and fonts.

- Chapter 2 is about the structure of a presentation and is a general overview of how to think the flow of your presentation. It's a key chapter.

- Chapter 3 discusses what you put on your slides: text and images.

- Chapter 4 is dedicated to editing images to make them suitable for a presentation.

- Chapter 5 talks about how to chain slides in the flow of a presentation. It may seem a trivial topic, but there is much to say about it.

- Chapter 6 discusses how to animate elements within a single slide.

- Chapter 7 explains how to combine animations and transitions to obtain a presentation that doesn't look like a PowerPoint presentation.

Appendices discuss short important topics:

- Introducing oneself, which, as it's usually the first thing you do in a presentation, gives the tone of the presentation.

- Licensing issues, with images in particular.

- Documents – what support to give to your audience? (Spoiler: not a printout of your slides.)

This book also comes with sample slides that implement the examples discussed in detail in the different chapters; the purpose of these slides is to enable you to run them and see by yourself the result. Sample slides are available for all chapters except the first and fourth ones, and can be downloaded from the source code page for this book at www.apress.com.

CHAPTER 1

■ ■ ■

Designing a Presentation

Recognizing the need is the primary condition for design.

—Charles Eames (1907-1978)

A speaker is always acutely sensitive to background noise coming between message and audience. I once had to give several days of technical training in a room overlooking the courtyard of a primary school, and recesses were tough. Yet, a surprising number of speakers seem to be unaware that some of the worst disturbances for an audience are visual ones, and could have been easily avoided. It's as painful for people at the back of the room to strain their eyes to try to decipher badly designed slides as it is for them to strain their ears to try to hear the speaker among the vigorous exercise outdoors of tiny but powerful lungs. At least, you know that recesses don't last forever, you can always pray for rain, and you cannot blame the speaker. Enduring a long presentation (and the worse the slides, the longer the presentation seems to be) of badly designed slides requires a solid amount of stoicism.

Surviving the Corporate Template

As a speaker, you have far more control over slide design than over outside disturbances. More control doesn't unfortunately always mean full control. If you work for a big company – and I have also had this problem in an educational institute – odds are that before you even think about the visual representation of what you want to say, the Graphical Charter and the mandatory PowerPoint Corporate Template will be forced upon you. Let me immediately say that I'm fully aware of the importance for a company of projecting a homogeneous image across its outside communications. Many technical presentations, though, are purely internal, and in this context I'm not persuaded that in an age that values diversity, a presentation that shares the same tired template as preceding presentations gets much help from design to make an impact.

Even in the case of a presentation to customers or, worse, prospective customers, I would advise you to polish your diplomatic skills and negotiate, from the start, trashing most of the corporate template with whomever can bless you with a go-ahead. Perhaps that my nomadic life as a consultant has given me a different perspective than if I had spent twenty years with the same company. Every corporate template looks to me desperately like every other corporate template; every unfamiliar logo looks to my eyes like any other logo. Even company names often look very much the same. If you are a small company trying to sell to a behemoth, trumpeting your "identity" from the start will impress no one. When you are far away from home, in an exotic place, all people look very much like clones. Make a friend there, and you would

Electronic supplementary material The online version of this chapter (doi:10.1007/978-1-4842-2295-9_1) contains supplementary material, which is available to authorized users.

immediately recognize that friend in a crowd. It's familiarity that breeds recognition. Repeating your logo on every page will not create familiarity with those who don't know you, and those who know you don't need it.

Most corporate PowerPoint templates seem to have been designed by people who have never presented before a live audience. My dislike of templates comes from their using a lot of screen space that I regard as precious. The example in Figure 1-1 comes from the sample "Training New Employees" PowerPoint presentation, and is supposed to be the "blank" slide. In practice, your playground will be the area I have shaded in yellow. I have computed the sizes with precision; the yellow area represents 63% of the full slide area. If you charitably include the area taken by the title into your playground, you painfully reach 78.5%.

Figure 1-1. *Space wasted by a template*

When you present in a large room, what is shown must be as big as possible so that people at the back can see. If you prepare a video that you expect a sizable part of the audience to watch over the screen of a smartphone, the problem is exactly the same. Better not start by reducing the usable surface by more than 20% and possibly up to 40%.

Even when I'm not using the full surface, I want emptiness as breathing space, and I don't want to see it polluted by graphical elements, logos, and dates that don't belong to what I'm talking about. I'm also resolutely against numbering slides; you'll understand why later in this book.

I have seen several times in technical sales presentations before an important lead the name, and sometimes the logo, of the lead repeated from slide to slide; noise again. Your audience wants to know primarily whether you have understood their technical issues and whether your solution can fix them.

When such a "personalization" is associated with what are obviously company stock slides, the effect that is conveyed is rather the opposite of the intent. There are better and more convincing ways of showing that you care for your potential customer's problems.

Similarly, I don't see the point in the frequent habit at conferences of repeating the conference name in the footer of the slides. It's sometimes a requirement of the conference organizers, and it makes sense in slides distributed as a kind of "proceedings" but not in a live presentation. Additionally, most people in the conference circuit recycle their presentations a number of times – which is an excellent thing, because the more people see a good and interesting presentation, the better. Give me an empty page; even a copyright notice doesn't belong to what you show, only to the documents that you leave behind. In a video, the copyright notice doesn't need to appear continuously. Do you see a permanent copyright notice in a feature film?

You can, and probably must, keep from a corporate template a few important elements. The color scheme and fonts are usually quite acceptable and usable. You can keep the title slide. If there is a final slide, you can certainly keep it as well and triumphantly display your company's logo – if your presentation was good, your company will no longer be alien and then your "identity" will be remembered. In between, all you need is a blank slate.

Speaking from experience, getting in a corporate context a free rein with the inner design of your presentation may be hard. You can probably convince people, though, that if the style becomes a handicap for presenting the content, it's style, not content, that must change. In the worst case, as a proof of concept, prepare a clean presentation, and apply the mandatory theme to a copy; the comparison between the two versions should be convincing enough.

I'm going to suppose in the following pages that we have no particular Corporate design constraints, but I'll try to stress what looks important to me (and why), so that if you have these constraints you know where to compromise and where to stand fast.

The Important Choices

Designing your slides means deciding on four important elements: what will be the format of your slides, which will be your main colors, what will be your background, and which fonts (with an s) you will be using. Although those four choices might be considered as pure form and somewhat secondary, it's extremely hard to change some of them at a later stage, and they may also affect your choice of a picture when you hesitate between several possibilities (the general tonality of a picture may harmonize better with your colors). Additionally, and that's the justification for corporate templates in spite of their flaws, slide design represents the image of your company – or your own personality. You should think about the general looks of your slides around the same time as you are defining the outline of your presentation.

Slide Size

The slide size is the ratio of the width to the height. I had never given much conscious thought to this aspect of slide design, until the day when I was asked to adapt one of my courses to, guess what, a template that was in a different size. Changing the theme colors of an existing presentation usually requires adjustment at a few places where contrast looks bad all of a sudden. Changing a font may cause text to wrap around in boxes and impact a handful of animations. Changing the slide size is horrible. Objects will look poorly placed, some figures and images will be distorted, and almost every slide will have to be manually altered. In my case I solved the problem through diplomatic skills, and retained my original layout. If there is one original commitment that shapes the future of your slide deck, it's the size.

The traditional choice is between 4:3, and the "widescreen" 16:9 format (other formats such as 16:10 size can also be available). Figure 1.2 shows a 4:3 dotted rectangle inside a 16:9 rectangle that is itself inside a 4:3 figure (I have doubly nested so that it's easier to see how each format may look on a screen that has the other format).

Figure 1-2. *Choosing a slide size*

Several factors can come into play. One is the expected medium on which your slides will be shown; you can try to fit the medium. It seems wiser to me to base your choice of a format on your subject. Whenever you explain something, you must avoid saying "as you have seen on the previous slide." Backward references will not help viewers who may just have had a moment of absence. There is a balance to maintain between avoiding clutter and having every important bit on the screen when you refer to it. What you'll have on your screen and how it will be laid out depends very much on your topic. Let me give a few examples.

When I have to show computer programs or database queries, I prefer using the 4:3 format because lines of code are usually relatively short, but I wish to show as many of them as possible to show complete functionalities. I believe that if I had to give a math lecture, with proofs, I would choose the same size. If I were going to talk about chemistry with chemical equations to balance, I'd rather choose a wider format. Many technical presentations are based on schemas that weren't created by the speaker in the first place. Are these schemas more horizontal, which would hint at a 16:9 size, or more vertical, which a 4:3 format would suit better? Another frequent element of a technical presentation is a time line, whether to express a flow or milestones in a project. Do you rather see the time axis as horizontal, or as vertical? I must stress that there is no right or wrong answer to the choice of a format; it really depends on how you envision what you have to talk about, because the full exercise is about transmitting this vision to your audience. You can always fit whatever you want to say into any format. Some people overcome surface and shape constraints; when given the uninspiring ceiling of a chapel to decorate or a block of marble to sculpt, Michelangelo usually managed rather well. For those of us who are considerably less talented, deciding ahead about how your presentation will globally look can save a number of headaches. One point worth noting though: usually photographs are in a 4:3 format. If you settle for a wide format and want pictures as a background (I will talk more about images in later chapters), reframing might in some cases be slightly delicate.

Color Palette

The palette is the set of colors that you'll use in your presentation. PowerPoint wants ten basic colors that it will further decline into five shades each, from lighter to darker. In practice, you rarely need more than four or five colors, to which you can possibly add black and white. If you have any say in the matter, the choice of the color palette is another important decision; as mentioned earlier, it can influence your choice of images, as you'll probably look for images that will harmonize well with what accompanies them.

If you're planning to talk abroad, I'd like to remind you that colors are culturally important, especially in Asia, where the symbolism of colors is different from Europe or the United States. It's well known, for instance, that red, which often means danger in Western cultures or in the Middle East, is a positive, lucky, and joyful color in China, where a red arrow pointing down sends an ambiguous message. Additionally, and this is true anywhere, colors may be associated with some religious or political movements and passions may be running high. Some technically excellent choices may be particularly unfortunate. Research seriously the subject before settling on a palette, and try to get the opinion of a native or someone perfectly familiar with the culture.

Most books that talk about presentations contain a small chapter on color theory, which explains that for color harmony you can choose either analogous colors, next to each other on a 12-color wheel; or complementary colors, on opposite sides of the wheel; or perhaps triads, with a triangle over the wheel and the colors at the angles; or ... I have never understood anything about color theory and I have always felt as clueless after reading a chapter on that topic as I was before starting it. There are so many options that you get a feeling that anything goes, when you know very well that it isn't so. Fortunately there are some excellent websites and tools to help you choose your colors.

Playing Corporate

If your presentation is in a company (or university) context, and if you haven't been blessed with a mandatory color palette, you can prove how good a team player you are by selecting one that does its bit for subtly heralding your company's identity. I'm going to illustrate it with the publisher of this book, Apress.

If you have a required title slide, save it as an image. Alternatively (this is what I'm going to do for Apress), take a screenshot of the home page of the corporate website, which you can do with a number of tools. We are going to pull our palette from this screenshot.

The first option that, to render unto John McWade what belongs to John McWade, derives from a method I found in his warmly recommended book *How To Design Cool Stuff*, consists in pixelizing this screenshot. Image manipulation programs such as Gimp, which we'll see in more detail in Chapter 4, propose a number of filters to alter images, among which filters that blur an image. Blurring options often propose "pixelization," in other word turning the image into a checkerboard of monochromatic squares that average the color of the actual pixels they replace (PowerPoint also provides image filters, but there is no pixelization in my version).

Figure 1-3 shows what the Apress home page looked like at the time of writing, and, what the Gimp pixelization turned it into, with two different square sizes. I based the choice of the square size on the original width of the screenshot, which was 1,000 pixels (I have adjusted it to be a round number), so the square size in is one case 1/25th of the image width and 1/50th in the other case. It's better to experiment with several sizes. As you can see, as colors are averaged, they become more muted as the square size increases. The best option is probably to pick brighter and darker colors from a transformation that uses small squares, and muted colors from a transformation that uses bigger squares. Now, how are we going to use these colors? We need one color for the background, one for text, and the other colors will be used for accenting what is important or perhaps coloring shapes that will be used in visual explanations. The master word for selecting background and text colors is "contrast."

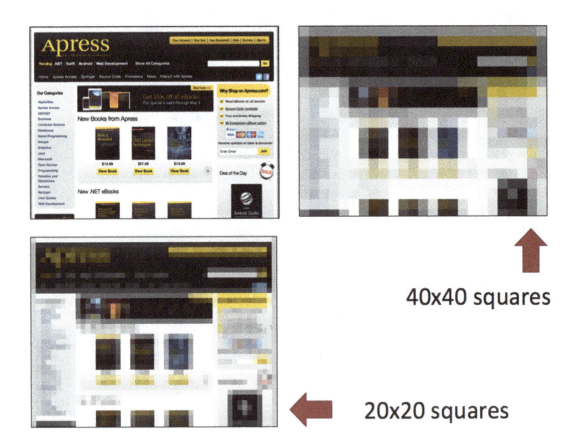

Figure 1-3. *Deriving a Palette from the Apress website*

In the Middle Ages the unavailability of spectacles led to a common understanding: to spare the short-sighted the painful experience of getting hit in the face with a flail when wandering on the wrong side, all warring parties would display distinctive signs that anybody could see well from a safe distance. Heraldry was born. Heraldry, besides a lot of funny words to describe *tinctures*, or colors, has rules. Tinctures are divided into *metals* (*or*, in other words, gold or yellow; and *argent*, in other words, silver or white), and *colours* (yes, with a u) called *gules* (red), *sable* (black), *azure* (blue), *vert* (green), and *purpure* (purple-ish red). There are also furs, which are more like patterns and irrelevant to our topic. Colours and metals are shown in Figure 1-4, together with, as an example, the coats of arms of the first eight Swiss cantons.

The key rule, which isn't always followed, is that you should always have a metal over a colour or the reverse, and never directly metal on metal or colour on colour. In Figure 1-4, two coats of arms don't fully respect the rule, the one of Urserental (fourth from the left, green background) and the one of Glarus on the right-hand side. When you look at the bottom of Figure 1-4, how the coats of arms look in shades of gray, you see that, especially from a distance, the black bear of Urserental vanishes in the background and the coat of arms is saved by the *argent* cross. The walking saint figure of Glarus remains a bit more legible, but his saving grace comes from the touches of *argent* and *or* that remove much of the guessing.

Figure 1-4. *The tinctures of heraldry*

Heraldic rules are rules that you can stick to; national flags follow them; when you have red over blue or the reverse, as in the British or Norwegian flag, there is white to separate them. Interestingly, you'll also note that black is a colour and isn't supposed to go over blue, green, or red, a rule that is often forgotten in presentations.

You will be no doubt pleased to discover that the Apress logo, being *or* over *sable*, plays by the rules. Pick two contrasted colors (metal and colour), one for the background, one for text, and use other colors for accent.

In the present enlightened days, contrast, of course, can be mathematically computed. You can find formulae, as well as an online tool to test color combinations, at `http://www.had2know.com/technology/color-contrast-calculator-web-design.html`.

I suspect that the same formulae are at work in the second option to extract a palette from a home page (or, for that matter, any image), which is using the tools at `https://color.adobe.com/`. Registration (it's free) allows you to upload any image and to automatically extract a palette from it. In fact, it allows you to extract several palettes, as you can specify a "mood." These palettes are not created by merely averaging colors, but by extracting what we might call representative pixels. An option also allows you to customize your palette by selecting pixels according to your personal affinity with them. Figure 1-5 shows the palettes that were automatically suggested to me by the tool from the Apress home page screenshot, as well as one I handcrafted from the same image. It may not seem obvious in the figure, but in my custom palette the lighter color isn't white; it's the background color for the menu on the left-hand side of the home page. I'll talk about white very soon. Take notice that automatic extraction isn't always as corporate minded as yourself: the blue in the third palette from the top looks like "Pay with American Express" blue or "Follow us on Twitter" blue, but not as Apress blue, and was probably picked from one of the icons present on the web page. In the same way, the red in the second palette seems to have been extracted from payment icons. Automatic extraction is a good point to start from, but has to be watched because of the possible presence of alien elements.

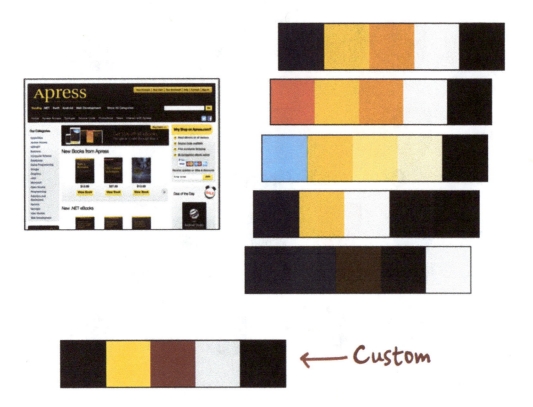

Figure 1-5. *Using the online Adobe tools to extract a palette*

Playing Solo

If you are representing nobody but yourself, or if you want to inject more of your own personality in your presentation, which is commendable, there is another option. This option uses features available on the same site I have just mentioned, `http://color.adobe.com`, where you must go to "explore," and it doesn't require any registration. Another good site, `http://www.colourlovers.com/`, offers similar features – the **u** in *colour* here is because the website is British, and doesn't refer to heraldry. You don't know which colors to choose? Type the name of a country, region, or city that you like or dream that you'll visit one day, a place that matches your tastes and your personality. Alternatively, you can also try the title of a film or book, or the name of a famous painter – anything you feel some affinity with. Search, and see what you find. Favor a palette that contains both dark and light colors (although adding black or white to a palette is always an option) and that would still look good in shades of gray. If you hesitate, as palettes are user rated, pick the best-loved one. You have your colors.

On color.adobe.com if you click on the palette then on "Edit," you'll see the codes that define colors. You get the information by simply clicking on the palette on colourlovers.com.

Whether you pick corporate colors or simply colors that reflect your tastes and personality, I think it is useful to relate them to heraldic tinctures. Put on the one side the metals, on the other side the colour, and respect the rules. Figure 1-6 shows my pick for a hypothetical Apress presentation, with colors I took mostly from my custom palette in Figure 1-5, completed by some colors from the automatic palettes.

Figure 1-6. *A possible Apress palette*

I have represented the color code inside each rectangle, and the color used for this color code is #0d0d0d on the left and #f2f2f2 on the right. Distinction between metal and colour isn't always as clear-cut as we'd like it to be – the bottom metal color is orange; is it closer to yellow or to red? Some colors sit somewhat on the fence. You can use them carefully, or drop them, or only use lighter or darker shades that belong clearly to one side or the other.

Although you should stick to your palette, there are cases when you may want to use what PowerPoint calls *Standard Colors*. I occasionally use some of them to display computer code. Many development environments automatically change the color of words or signs that they recognize and that have a special meaning in a programming language. The purpose is to help notice typos quickly. My palette doesn't always contain colors that are close enough to those my audience may be familiar with, and when this happens, I pick standard colors.

I've been using here hexadecimal codes (base 16) that are commonly used to specify colors on web pages. The first two characters represent a quantity of red, the two next ones a quantity of green, and the two last ones a quantity of blue, hence the RGB acronym usually associated with these codes. Hexadecimal RGB values can be directly entered in PowerPoint, as you'll see at the end of this chapter. In LibreOffice, you enter separately decimal values for red, green, and blue. The calculator on your computer usually has a Programmer option that lets you easily convert between hexadecimal and decimal values.

Slide Background

In my view, the background should be as plain, I'd almost say as dull, as possible. It's the foreground, not the background, which must be interesting. In the same way it's a painting that should attract your attention, not its frame. If you want perfect examples of what *not* to use, look on the web with any search engine for images corresponding to "slide background." The result will be flamboyant. To the pedagogical reason of trying to put the focus where it belongs, I can add a technical one: a fancy background, and in my book even a gradient is fancy, will seriously limit your options with an interesting method that I'll introduce in Chapter 5; in most cases, it will completely prevent you from using it. You are warned.

Pick one of the lightest metals and one of the darkest colours from your palette. One will be for the background, the other one for default text. The only worthy debate for me is this: dark on a light background or light on a dark background? Opinions diverge, and it depends on circumstance. Dark backgrounds, and more particularly dark blue backgrounds, are perennial favorites of professional conferences. Dark backgrounds also look great on the giant TV screens you often find in the meeting rooms of large companies. However, when your audience is normally expected to take notes, and I'm thinking specifically about lectures, if you lower the ambient light in the screen area of the room to improve visibility from the back, there may be very little light available for note takers in the first ranks (some people, incredibly, still take notes by hand). Additionally, if you like striding before the screen in the path of the projection, most of your audience will remember you as a kind of giant Smurf.

I also believe that for difficult light conditions (for instance a glorious sun outside and a window than cannot be obscured because of a stuck blind, this kind of situation happens), a light background should remain a tad more legible. You have understood that I have a slight preference for a light background, but I mostly regard it as a matter of taste.

I wish to specify that when I say light, I really mean light, perhaps even very light, but not pure white. You would probably not use a black background, yet a black background may be better than a white one. Unless you are presenting at a conference for mountain guides and they all came with their glacier goggles, a white background soon becomes blinding. If the lighter non-white color in your palette still feels too dark to you, there are a number of online tools on the web (I can mention for instance `http://www.colllor.com` or `http://www.hexcolortool.com`) where you can enter the code of your color and obtain the codes for various shades, either darker or lighter ones. This a good way to obtain a whiter shade of pale that will still harmonize with the remainder of your palette.

The last important design element is the choice of fonts.

Fonts

If you want to give homogeneity to your presentation, you must also define which fonts you will use. Fonts with an s, because it's very likely that you will need several different fonts. Typically, if you need to show mathematical formulae as sometimes happens in scientific talks, you may find a calligraphic font suitable for function and variable names. For the topics I usually talk about – information systems, databases, and programming, I really need three fonts: one for regular text, one for program code, and a font that simulates handwriting for annotations or asides. I frequently use annotations (of which you have a sample in Figure 1-5 and in the next figures). I have seen some great lectures where the lecturer was presenting regular slides and was annotating them using a tablet as he was talking; but I saw them on YouTube. In a live presentation, that would mean being seated behind the desk and not moving from there during the lecture. This is acceptable in a relatively small room. In a large auditorium, I like to move and occupy the space rather than stay put in a corner, and not using anything but a remote control to advance my slides or trigger animations. Additionally, you have to remember everything that isn't in your slides, and sometimes you may have to talk when you aren't at your best – suffering from jet lag, worried by personal issues, or simply unwell – and forget part of your script. A mock annotation will act as a prompter. Using a handwritten script (which isn't the easiest one to read from afar, so use it lightly) gives a completely illusory personal touch, and a feeling of spontaneity to a carefully prepared presentation.

Once again, choosing a font is not all about selecting whichever default your computer proposes. Traditionally, fonts are classified into the following:

- Serif fonts such as Times Roman that have little strokes (called serifs) attached and are perfect for small lines in a book;

- Sans serif fonts that haven't these strokes ("sans" means "without" in French), such as Arial;

- Monospace fonts, in which all letters occupy the same width, such as Courier New;

- and one or several categories such as "Cursive," "Decorative," "Script," "Fancy," which welcome any font that doesn't fit squarely into one of the other categories. Comic Sans MS is an example of such a font.

Figure 1-7 shows a number of fonts that you find almost anywhere (plus the font that I use for annotations, which is a free font by Denise Chan called *Ampersand*).

You'll read everywhere that for a presentation you must use a sans serif font. Typography is a complicated science, with a history that goes all the way back to Gutenberg in the 15th century, and which is constantly adapting to the modern world and to reading increasingly being from screens rather than printed paper. As a result, the simple advice needs to be qualified.

The important point is that text remains legible even from the top of the auditorium, or when written small on a mobile device. Letters must not only be simple (which is the reason for shunning traditional serif fonts), but they must have little *emphasis*, which is a technical term that means that some parts in a letter are far thicker than others. Emphasis is very smart and looks classy on a wedding invitation, but is terrible for a presentation because from afar thin parts disappear. The uppercase A in Book Antiqua or the Gs in Georgia clearly show emphasis in Figure 1-7. There are, though, other aspects to notice in Figure 1-7. Even if I have given the same size (40) to all text blocks, Verdana (especially), Georgia, and Lucida Console all look bigger than the surrounding fonts. Although it isn't officially qualified as a serif font, Courier New *is* a serif font, and Comic Sans MS, as its name says, is a sans serif font. Comic Sans MS also looks terribly cheesy to many people, and must be one of the most hated of all fonts. Avoid it like the plague, even if I have seen it used more than once in an academic context. In the professional world, Comic Sans MS is usually synonymous with amateurish, not "informal and friendly" as usually intended by people who pick it.

Figure 1-7. *Some common fonts*

Other than serif and emphasis, another important characteristic of a font is its width. One of the numerous things I have learned from John McWade is that the larger the font size, the closer letters should be, and the converse is true. I don't know exactly why, perhaps that there is some kind of ideal scope that our eyes can grasp, but you can easily verify this assertion by trying to read the cast from a small format movie poster. The width is a very interesting point, because many recent fonts have been created to make reading easier on small electronic devices, which means that they are wide. In a presentation, you want big letters to make them legible for the people at the back. Usually, I consider that the comfort range is between sizes 24 and 36 included for regular text. Bigger, it starts looking like a title. I may have to get down to 20 because of intractable layout issues with program code, but I try to avoid it. As your letters are big, you want them relatively packed for visual comfort. I have in Figure 1-8 written the same text, in the same size (32), using the different fonts in Figure 1-7 (including Comic Sans MS). This figure explains why replacing a font with another sometimes breaks carefully crafted alignments.

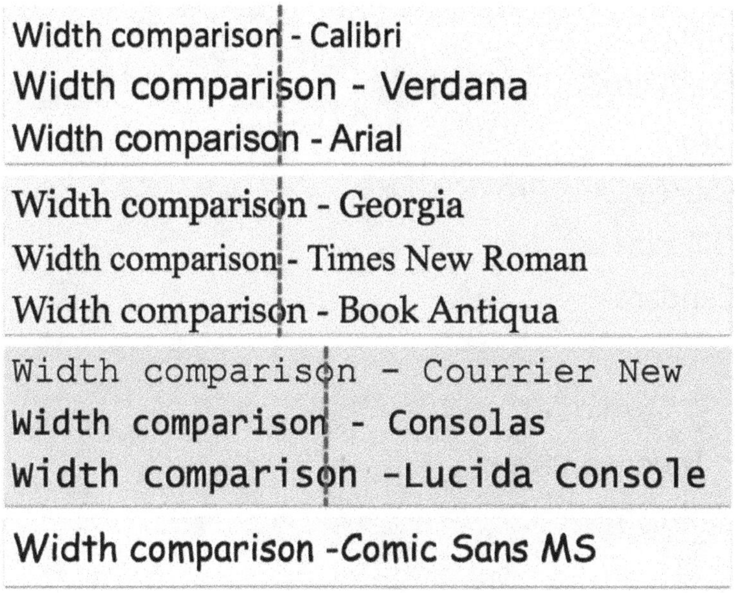

Width comparison - Calibri
Width comparison - Verdana
Width comparison - Arial

Width comparison - Georgia
Width comparison - Times New Roman
Width comparison - Book Antiqua

Width comparison - Courrier New
Width comparison - Consolas
width comparison -Lucida Console

Width comparison -Comic Sans MS

Figure 1-8. *Width comparison with various common fonts*

You can immediately spot that Verdana, for instance, was designed for making small text legible. It's a poor choice for slides, for which Calibri is better, which explains why it's the PowerPoint default (at least in my version). In the same way, Consolas is a far better font for showing computer code than Courier New (which you see often), because it's narrow and it's mostly a sans serif font (as all letters occupy the same space, very narrow letters have serifs to make them look wider and avoid unpleasant visual gaps).

When selecting fonts, there is an important practical question: will you present on the same computer that you are using to prepare the presentation, or not? In theory, you can save fonts with presentations; in practice I have had lots of unpleasant surprises and carefully crafted presentations that looked misaligned because of an unexpected font substitution. Some fonts have license restrictions that prevent them from being saved with your slides. Switching from Windows to Mac or the reverse is also likely to mess up everything as you may discover some slight differences in fonts. If there are high odds that you will be presenting on another computer (projection equipment is sometimes moody, especially when your computer comes from another continent), don't take any risk and stay with arch-classic fonts; or save your fonts to a USB stick and be prepared to install them on another computer. The fonts I have shown in Figures 1-7 and 1-8 are more or less available everywhere and aren't risky choices.

If you are certain that you will run the presentation on your own computer and if using the same fonts as everybody else is unappealing to you, then you can opt for fonts that are classical fonts but not the ones commonly used by the hoi polloi. Give preference to fonts for which a large number of styles are available; mixing the styles of a single font allows for emphasis in an unobtrusive way. Franklin Gothic and Amble (a bit wide for my taste) are for instance in this respect excellent choices. Make sure that every accented character that you need is present in case you need to write in a language other than English or Dutch; some fonts only provide unaccented Latin characters.

Figure 1-9 shows some (free) alternative choices to the standard ones, once again at size 32. There are many sans serif fonts that are almost as tight as Calibri. Differences can usually be found in the shape of some letters such as *a* or *g*. For monospace fonts, you see that you can easily find tighter than Consolas; I generally use Inconsolata for showing computer code.

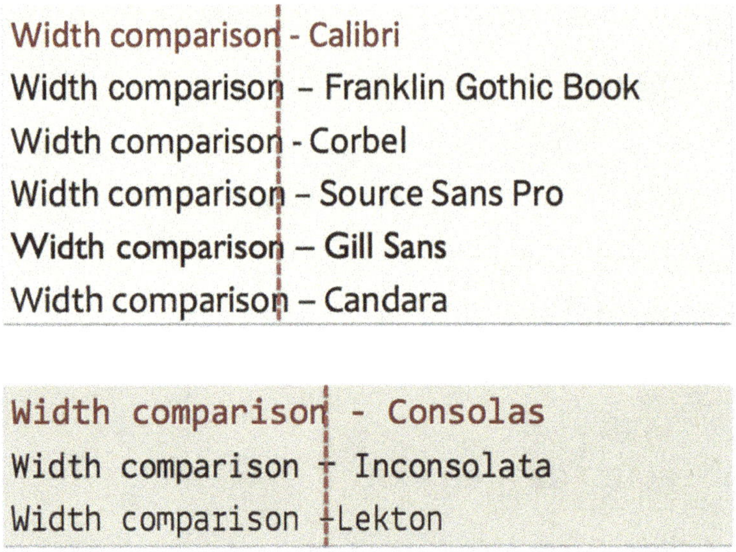

Width comparison - Calibri

Width comparison – Franklin Gothic Book

Width comparison - Corbel

Width comparison – Source Sans Pro

Width comparison – Gill Sans

Width comparison – Candara

Width comparison - Consolas

Width comparison – Inconsolata

Width comparison –Lekton

Figure 1-9. *Alternate less standard fonts*

There are a few free fonts sites that I am particularly fond of.

One is moorstation.org. Click on the typoasis link, then visit (more particularly) the "themes" section, full of interesting fonts, especially under "Timeless Beauties."

You'll also find good fonts at fontsquirrel.com, with very clear licensing rights, as well as at fontlibrary.org.

I also feel, in spite of what you read everywhere, that some serif fonts with no emphasis and discreet serifs such as Cambria can also be used. I have done it a few times.

Generally speaking, avoid fonts that are too fancy. For professional conferences, where attendees often expect both to learn and to be entertained, you can sometimes give a theme to your presentation (as in "theme park"), in which case the base font may be unusual. Even so, always think about legibility and the people at the back of the room. In sales presentations and lectures, be as sober as you can be – as you'll see in the next chapter, it doesn't mean that you'll never be fancy in your presentation.

Saving the Theme

At this stage, you can start preparing a "theme" that will include your main font and your colors, and save this theme. This will ensure some minimal consistency in a series of presentations such as a series of lectures, the different parts of a seminar, or a number of technical sales presentations focused on different products offered by your company. Creating a theme is a bit tedious, but it will save you a lot of time later.

In PowerPoint, open a new presentation and click on either the "Design" or the "Themes" tab (it can be named differently depending on your version of PowerPoint). This is where you will define your slide size, as well as default colors, fonts, and background.

As soon as your slide size is set, start with the colors. Figure 1-10 shows my definition of the "Apress Theme," using my custom palette and completing all the other colors with colors from the various possible palettes we have seen. The only colors I haven't changed are those related to hyperlinks.

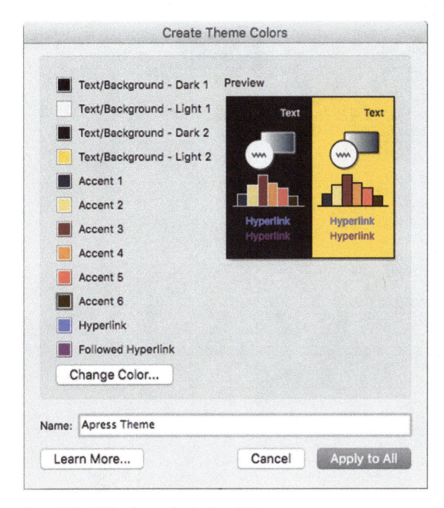

Figure 1-10. *Adding theme colors in PowerPoint*

The easiest way to enter colors after clicking on "Change Color …" is to use the RGB sliders tab and directly enter the color codes provided by color websites. You can always slightly modify colors. Moving sliders to the right will lighten colors, and moving sliders to the left will darken them.

When all colors have been set, give a name to the theme and click on "Apply to All."

In LibreOffice, in the menu click on "Format," then "Area," then the colors tab. You can define colors one by one then add them as shown in Figure 1-11.

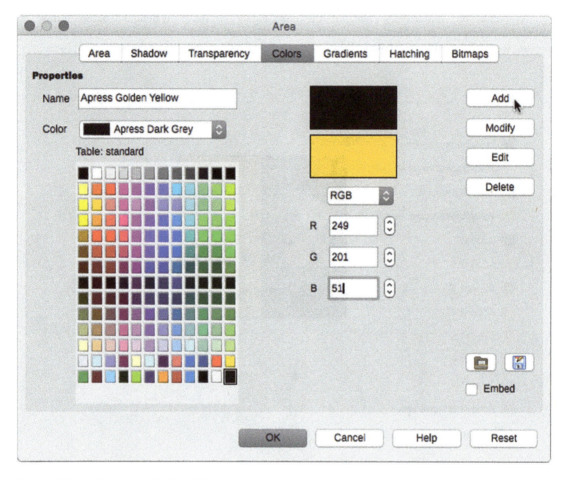

Figure 1-11. *Adding colors in LibreOffice Impress*

Once you are done with colors, you should set the background color. It's one of the options in the "Theme" or "Design" tab in PowerPoint; for LibreOffice Impress you must click on the "Styles and Formatting" icon on the right-hand side (the wrench), then the "Presentation style" icon at the top of the area that appears; "Background" is in the list, right-click on it.

Changing fonts basically means hunting down in the various options every element where text may appear (especially under "Drawing Object Styles" in LibreOffice Impress). It's less tedious with PowerPoint.

Finally, save as a template. With PowerPoint it's a special format that you must select when saving the document, with LibreOffice Impress you must select "Templates" under the "File" menu option. Then you are set and it's time to think about the flow of your presentation.

Summary

In this chapter we covered the following:

- Templates often consume a lot of space in your visuals for no benefit.

- Always think of the guy at the back of the room.

- You must give some unity to your presentations through design, but by a careful choice of slide size, which should depend on your topic; your palette of colors, including the background that is better left plain; and a few fonts that are easy to read from afar and in which letters aren't widely spaced.

We have seen how each slide should look; let's turn now to how they should look together.

CHAPTER 2

■ ■ ■

The Score

Hvor ord svigter, taler musikken.

Where words fail, music speaks.

—Hans-Christian Andersen (1805-1875)

The most important element in a presentation is, of course, not how it looks, even if bad looks can obscure a message, but what it says, and how it says it. The key issue when delivering a message is making its important points stick into the minds of the audience, when you know very well that they won't be able, how hard you try, to retain everything any more than you would in their place. Numerous studies have been carried out showing that the average attention span is anywhere between ten and twenty minutes; of course, attention level comes and goes, and people may pay attention to you again once they have checked their email or posted on the Net what they think of your presentation. If you cannot expect people to stay focused much longer than fifteen minutes, and if your presentation is longer than this span, the real difficulty is therefore to be able to spur attention when it needs a boost. I'll try to define broad principles in this chapter; implementation and details will come in later chapters of this book.

Storytelling

Because stories are memorable, most authors who write about presentations emphasize the story line, with frequent references to Hollywood. The argument goes like this: everybody likes a story, so you need a script that tells a story, in the tried and tested Hollywood fashion. An initial situation, an event, a string of adventures till a climax, resolution, and a happy end. Preferably with clearly identified good and bad guys ("guy" being of course a metaphor).

However, and more specifically in the area of technical and scientific presentations, I'm not sure that the Hollywood treatment can always be applied. At a professional conference, where you are more or less free to talk about whatever you want as long as it fits the theme of the conference and your paper was accepted, you can in many cases build your talk around an anecdote. Unfortunately, the more technical you get, and it happens at professional conferences as well, the more difficult storytelling becomes. An article in *Nature* a few years ago was researching the most quoted scientific papers. I assume that presentations were associated with each of them, and, to only take the top three most quoted papers, I must say that I remain a bit perplexed about how to apply Hollywood-style scripting to biological lab techniques such as these:

- *Protein measurement with the folin phenol reagent,*

- *Cleavage of structural proteins during the assembly of head of the bacteriophage T4,*

- *A rapid and sensitive method for the quantitation of microgram quantities of protein utilizing the principle of protein-dye binding.*

Perhaps that the second paper could be turned into something such as *The Night of the Bacteriophages* but I fear that it would be going a bit too far.

Another piece of good advice that I have seen is that if you haven't any natural story line, you can paint a vivid picture of life without what you are trying to sell (in the wider sense) to your audience, then with it, and show how better it is with than without. It's an excellent idea if you have a product or service for sale and are pitching – the setting, the problem, and tada! Your product arrives and saves the world (you'll notice that it's basically a bad guy/good guy story). Such an outline can also work pretty well for a talk at a professional conference, where you often speak about your experience and how you solved issues that will resonate with most of your audience. It becomes harder in a university context. It's challenging to raise interest among students for solutions to problems that they are discovering at the same time; when students have no experience of how bad the bad guy can be, they have no particular sympathy for the good guy.

Irrespective of the background of your audience, if you can build a relatively short presentation around a story, it's far more difficult in a context of training or education over several days, weeks or months, when you cannot really drag a story on and on like some TV series. When instructing people, you have to stick to a course description or to a curriculum; some parts of it make for good story material, and other parts far less so. It's not easier to have a story with presentations on a theme such as "new features in the last version of this well-known software product"; you can try to build a story around each feature, but it may not be very consistent as a whole. Additionally, some stories may be far better than others. What I fear most in a training session or a series of lectures is when I come to a list of items that as an instructor I don't find particularly exciting but that I feel, or was told that, I have to talk about: standards, built-in functions, the new features I was just mentioning, whatever can quickly degenerate into a boring catalogue.

Even when you are presenting a single well-defined topic, it happens that neither the classic Hollywood script nor the "before … and now …" kind of story really applies. Many people will no doubt be disappointed, but honesty forces me to admit that there wasn't in my life a "before the Bolzano-Weierstrass theorem" and a "after the Bolzano-Weierstrass theorem." I must even confess that I hurried to forget how little I ever knew about compactness and convergent subsequences.

Don't misread me: I believe in the power of stories, and I'll come back to them in this chapter. However, I often feel that looking for a story, in a classical sense, as the backbone for a technical presentation isn't the best way to develop and build the presentation; the story doesn't always work. I find it easier to consider what I want to say, define what I consider the key messages, and try to organize my presentation so as to highlight these key messages. I prefer thinking about my presentation more as a piece of music than as a single story, with a theme and rhythm – elements that are also visually present in a good film, although less obvious than the plot itself. This is why I'm referring in this chapter to a "score."

Orchestration

Even when you have no obvious plot for your presentation, you can always think of it as a piece of visual music; it can be a short one, a longer one that you have to break into movements, or the quasi-Wagnerian operatic cycle of a series of lectures. In music and in presentations, there is nothing duller than mechanical repetition. If so many presentations are boring, it's because they are so predictable – five bullet points, next slide, five bullet points, next slide … Even when speakers try to lighten up their slides, standard clipart that you have already seen in umpteen presentations becomes one more predictable, and therefore boring, element. Some very talented speakers, through presence, passion, and charisma, manage to pull it through, even with a poor slide deck. Many speakers get drawn by the mechanical rhythm imposed by their slides, and the presentation becomes like Shakespearean verse recited by school kids, minus indulgent parents. Very soon, people who are still awake in the audience stop paying attention and the message no longer flows from the speaker to them.

Continuity and Breaks

Giving rhythm to a presentation has two prerequisites: solidly establishing a "standard," the global design issues that have been discussed in the previous chapter contribute to it; and then departing from this standard whenever you need to wake up your audience. If you want to trick your audience into paying attention, you must first teach them what to expect next, and at the right point surprise them with something that deviates from expectations. Breaks cannot go without continuity: if the presentation has no recognizable style in the general sense, any variation will pass unnoticed and the effect will be lost. The standard, and the continuity that you can give to a presentation, is like the "basso continuo" (continuous bass) of Baroque music, the recurring theme of a symphony, or the rhythm section of a Jazz band or the bass and drums of rock. If you prefer films to music, there are remarkable examples about continuity and breaks in Bruce Block's *The Visual Story*.

Continuity in Slides

If the general design of your presentation contributes to continuity, continuity isn't only about global looks. Consistency must also be strictly maintained. When I speak about computer science or information technology, I often have to talk about processes (as in "operating system process"). It doesn't matter whether I represent them as squares, round-cornered squares, ellipses, or circles; I just need to be consistent in my representation. Colors also need to be very consistent: when you assign a special color to some text or shape that represents something special, keep it. Don't look for variety now; we'll introduce variety, but later and with a purpose. Try to have Wagnerian-like leitmotivs; in a Wagner opera a short musical phrase is associated with each character. In the same way, try to give a specific visual identity to every important concept that will appear several times in the course of your presentation; it can be a shape, a color, or an image always associated with the concept. Copy and paste from slide to slide. After the first explanation of the concept, people will recognize it easily when it comes back, even if it's an abstract idea.

Additionally, there is a strong dynamic element to continuity. A very important notion for me, and I'll come back to it several times in this book, is to stop thinking about "slides," and start thinking about "sequences."

One point that is essential but that few people seem to really understand is that the number of slides in a presentation is arbitrary. There are in presentation software two mechanisms that are strongly related: transitions (how you switch from the preceding slide to the current slide); and animations, which are about making elements appear, disappear, and move inside a slide. I'll talk about transitions and animations in far greater detail in the last chapters of this book, but I just want to say now that if they aren't strictly identical, there is much overlap, and depending on how you use them your number of slides may vary greatly. Let's illustrate it.

First of all, one of my core principles is to make objects appear on the screen, whether they are graphical elements or text, only when I'm ready to comment on them. Never let the audience run ahead of you. If I want to make appear three geometrical shapes one upon another, and if I have something special to say about each one of them, I'm not going to show them all at once. I'm going to show one, then the next one, then the last one. Figure 2-1 illustrates the two different ways that I can achieve this result. I can have a single slide with the second and third shapes that appear on a click as on the left-hand side in the figure, and in that case I use animation, or I can copy the slide two times with all three shapes, only to keep the first one on the first slide, the first two on the second slide, and everything on the third slide, then display one slide after the other, as on the right-hand side of the figure.

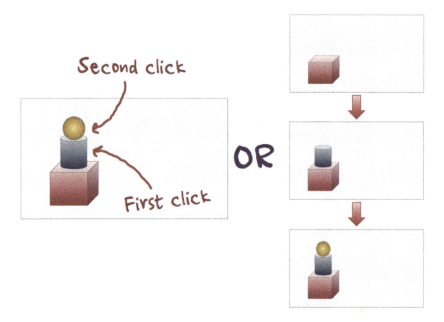

Figure 2-1. *Alternate ways of making elements appear on click*

Whether I use one slide or three slides, visually it will be identical. The only way the audience can tell what is really going on, is when the slide number changes if slides are numbered - which is why I don't number my slides. I prefer people to watch rather than try to guess from numbers how I did this or that.

What I'm showing here works of course as well with faded as with sudden appearances, and also with a few other ways of revealing elements that are available both as transitions or animations. I'm trying to demonstrate two points:

- First, choosing between transition and animation is in a number of cases a pure question of personal technique. I tend to combine both, and split across several slides when animations become too numerous on one slide.

- Second, as a consequence, thinking "slide" is completely meaningless.

Naturally, for a specific individual who uses a consistent style and a consistent technique, the number of slides **can** be meaningful. I know very well that when I talk for a lecture or a seminar I must plan for one slide per minute on average, with a couple animations per slide; but if I'm using a different style of presentation it can be very different. I once was given the instruction "20 minutes, 5 slides." I was precise almost to the second with duration, but I fired a broadside of 293 slides (one every 3 seconds on average; I wouldn't sustain that rhythm for two hours, nor would the audience); and yes, I was applauded. I had a particular reason for this hectic pace: this presentation was part of a "lunch and learn" session, and the IT managers who were attending it had an appetizing meal before them (it was in France). I had to keep them off their plates.

Generally speaking, a shorter talk will proportionally consume far more slides than a longer talk; for a short talk your audience will be fresh and focused (unless it's the last conference of the day), and you can have a more dynamic presentation. You also need more movement on the screen if your audience cannot see you. For a 10-minute video I'm usually close to 60 slides.

The commonly encountered advice "one idea per slide" is in my view a very bad one, because it drills into your mind this wrong notion that the slide is the unit, when what it actually says is that you should never have several ideas on the same slide. The slide is not the unit; the idea is the unit. Keep at least one element (other than the title or your logo in the footer) from one slide to the next, and your audience will see the other elements popping up or disappearing, not a slide change. It will be the same idea across several slides. Even when everything on the screen changes, you can maintain a visual sense of continuity. I've illustrated this point in Figure 2-2. There is nothing in common between Bremen in Germany on a very rainy day and the dream vacation spot at the bottom, except the presence of water and blue reflections; yet they fade effortlessly one into the other because I have carefully adjusted and reframed the two pictures so as to have the street level at the back of the first picture on the same spot as the horizon line in the second picture. The horizon becomes the element that provides continuity.

Figure 2-2. *Continuity when everything changes (pictures by Andreas Dantz and MattJP, found on Flickr)*

If you illustrate a point by using a sequence of slides, you must switch between slides as discreetly as possible. Exclude all fancy transitions, *especially* random ones. Keep to no transition (which is the default), and fades. The feeling of continuity comes from visual elements, which can be text, images, or lines as in Figure 2-2, which keep the same place in two successive slides. This feeling of continuity is reinforced if the static objects are strategically placed; I learned from Garr Reynolds that thirds, whether they are vertical or horizontal, are strength lines that draw attention. The third is far more powerful than the center. You'll notice in Figure 2-2 that the horizon line, which is the invariant element, is on the bottom third of the slide. It attracts your eyes, and you feel magically transported from a rainy street to a sunny island.

Breaking Continuity

It's only when continuity has been solidly established that you can think about breaks. Breaks have two functions: low-intensity breaks that simply mark a transition from an idea to another one, and high-intensity breaks that are signals to pay attention. A low-intensity break may simply be **not** keeping any element from one slide to the next, and having no transition at all – very much like a shot change in a film. Depending on how strongly you depart from what your audience expects, they will perceive the break more or less consciously.

To decide where breaks should go, your starting point should of course be a strong outline for your presentation; it could also be an older presentation to improve! Some people recommend a storyboard, which basically means drawing by hand everything on a piece of paper even before you switch your computer on. A storyboard is a good idea, but as it requires doing some of the work twice, once by hand and once using presentation software, it's perhaps more appropriate for high-stakes presentations. For a seminar or a series of lectures, I usually work on a script and a kind of PowerPoint draft where I try visual ideas, with numerous switches between the one and the other until everything converges.

When do we want to break, other than transitioning from one idea to the next? Whenever we want something to stick. You must identify the few points that you want to remain in your audience's mind. When I say "few," I actually mean "2 or 3," and the time scope is one continuous span of talk; if you are giving a seminar with intermissions, each intermission resets counters. You may hope that far more than three points will remain; but you need define the three most important ones. Once you know what they are, you should introduce a break not *on* them but *before* them. You should prepare your audience to receive important information, in the very same way that in a circus a drum roll prepares the audience to a part of a number that is particularly difficult or daring. Timing is important: the drum roll doesn't occur during the quintuple somersault, but before it, to give time to a blasé audience to focus their attention. In the very same way, breaks should immediately precede, as a drum roll, parts of your presentation that you want to be memorable.

You can introduce different types of breaks. First, you can change all of a sudden some of your design options. Let's see some possibilities offered by playing with the design:

- Changing the background color,

- Changing fonts,

- Changing other colors than the background.

Inverting the foreground and background colors as illustrated in Figure 2-3 is a sober yet very effective technique, which I have first seen used by Dick Hardt in his legendary *Identity 2.0* presentation. If you illustrate both good and bad practices, it makes identification immediate as soon as you have established, with your first example of something that you disapprove of, what are your visual codes. I also sometimes need an aside in a presentation: for instance, a refresher about notions that are supposed to be already known. In that case, I also change, in a less dramatic way than for a good practice/bad practice example, the background color; I may replace the lightest color in my palette with the second lightest one. It gives a different visual identity to a part that doesn't belong to the main flow of the presentation. I usually combine a background change and fancy transitions, which I'm going to discuss shortly. The idea is similar to flashbacks in films, which may be slightly out of focus or in which colors may have been de-saturated, thus getting a special visual identity. Even if the aside may not be an important point in your talk, its purpose, to put everybody on the same page, is important enough to make sure that it doesn't pass unnoticed.

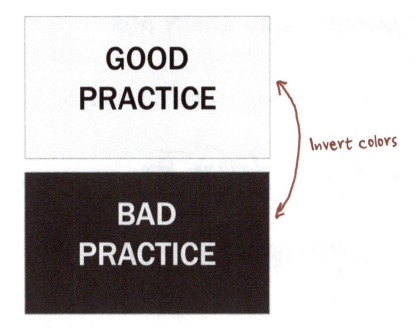

Figure 2-3. *Break by inverting background/foreground*

You can also play with fonts. If your base fonts should be most legible, a much less legible fancy font can be used to carry a particular message. The change of font will create a break. Forcing the audience to briefly strain their eyes to read an unfamiliar font may be a way to demand attention (beware that it's a dangerous game to play with an audience whose native alphabet isn't the Latin one – something too hard to read may quickly become undecipherable). Annotations in a mock handwritten script follow the same logic.
Figure 2-4 shows a number of examples of "messages" followed by the name of the font used to write them. Fonts associated with a well-known brand or a currently very successful film can also be used, but make sure with any kind of cultural reference that it's familiar to your audience. Blue, horizontally striped capital letters may resonate better with CIOs than with civil engineers or students.

BEWARE OF CONSEQUENCES - ROCKY AOE

the very old fashion way - CRY UNCIAL

The old fashion vvay - Aquiline Two

Mega-Important - Impact

Figure 2-4. *Unusual fonts for special messages*

Other colors than the background color can be changed to good effect. A plain, intense color that doesn't belong to your usual palette will be automatically noticed. One element in an unusual color begs for attention.

There are other manners to introduce a break in a presentation other than a sudden departure from the design standards. Some of them will catch attention in a hardly perceptible way; others will operate at a far more conscious level. I'll talk about technicalities later, but as I see most of these presentation elements as break opportunities, I want to talk very briefly about these:

- Images
- Quotes
- Movement
- Transitions

Images, especially in a technical presentation where people mostly expect diagrams or illustrative photographs, are an easy way to introduce a break, and they need to be both relevant and unexpected. Needless to say, be extremely careful with pictures in an international context, what is perfectly innocent or funny in one country can be perceived as in bad taste, risqué, or even offensive in another one.

Witty quotes can provide a good break too, provided, once again, that they are relevant. I prefer, in the course of a technical presentation, witty quotes to inspirational quotes, which are better used as a conclusion. Whenever I quote somebody, I associate the quote with a portrait of the author, which means that it's also an image. Try not to bring your audience to an unknown territory. Quote people they have at least heard of, and beware that fame is often circumscribed within national borders; if you are an American speaking in Britain or India, don't quote a famous baseball coach (if you want to hit a home run, you'd better refer to cricket – and you'd better avoid expressions such as "home run"). Historical figures, especially if they have had a huge impact on history and are nationalistic icons, can remain controversial for several centuries and are better quoted with extreme caution in an international context. Literary giants are usually safe (although there are better authors than Kipling to quote in India), so are great scientists. I'll talk more about images and quotes in the next chapter.

Movement, which will be covered extensively in Chapter 6, is also a very good way to introduce a break. Figure 2-5 illustrates how to animate a slide that would introduce exactly the types of break that I'm talking of right now – images, quotes, and movement - with the purpose of putting a special emphasis on movement:

- Make the "Images" text move in from the left, comment on the topic (which might be done with a few example slides before bringing back the slide illustrated in the figure).

- Then the "Quotes" text moves in from the left too, exactly like "Images," and is commented.

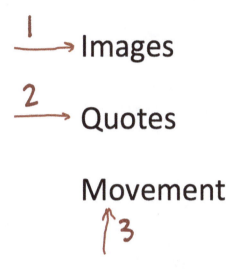

Figure 2-5. *Breaking movement continuity*

By now, empty space left at the bottom of the slide makes clear enough that a third point is coming, and everybody is expecting it to be introduced from the left as the two previous ones. Making "Movement" appear from the bottom introduces a modest element of surprise that goes against expectations and rekindles interest. The effect can be even stronger if you combine a movement break with a color change.

Finally, transitions, the main topic of Chapter 5, are an excellent way to manage an important break; by important break, I mean a change of topic, an aside, or the announcement of a coffee break in a seminar (very important). When you need an important break, you are going to interrupt the regular flow of slides. Normally, in the course of a presentation, I have two different ways to chain one slide to the next:

- Whenever I want continuity, either a fade or a substitution (no transition at all) and elements positioned at the same place in two successive slides,

- And when I want no continuity because I'm talking about a new idea, no transition and different elements at different places in the two successive slides.

Even when there is no continuity from one slide to the next, it's still the same flow, not a new chapter. Fades and substitutions are for me standard ways of chaining slides. As you'll see in Chapter 5, there are many possible transitions, and you can use a fancier transition to announce a new part. Such a fancier transition could be for instance a "push" transition in which you see the next slide (let's call it B) pushing away the current slide A. What I think is important is to use not once but twice the same fancy transition, but with symmetrical directions, as illustrated for an aside in Figure 2-6. In this example I have actually applied two breaks: a background change and a transition change, with a pair of symmetrical transitions bracketing the aside. If I had to announce a new part in my talk, I could have a single slide with the title for the new part between two symmetrical fancy transitions.

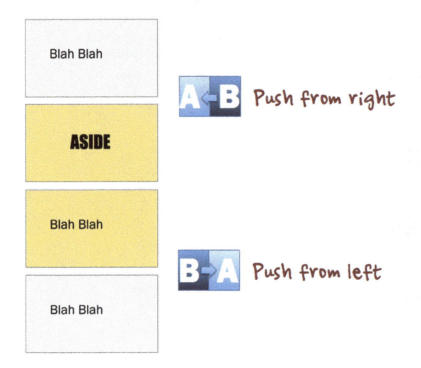

Figure 2-6. *Breaking transition continuity*

Use breaks sparingly: they are recognized as breaks only when continuity dominates.

Melody

After having defined a rhythm, it's time to talk about melody. I said at the beginning of this chapter that if I am dubious that every technical presentation can be turned into a Hollywood-style plot or even into a more basic "before … after …" story, I am nevertheless a strong believer in the power of stories. If building a technical presentation around a single story sometimes looks a bit constrained, in many cases stories and anecdotes come naturally in the course of your talk. Stories will not only give life to a presentation, they will also behave like mnemonics for each important point. For a technical sales presentation or a seminar, any experienced consultant will probably remember a few war stories. For a lecture, science is full of stories; mention Archimedes' principle or Newton's universal gravitation, and most people will think of Archimedes running out of his bath naked and shouting *Eureka!*, or of Isaac Newton brutally awaken from his nap by a falling apple. Stories really are like the melody that enriches your score.

As every technical presentation is different, I want to illustrate story and narration with a simple example: let's say that we want to talk about as exciting a topic as the intercept theorem. If you search the web for presentations of the intercept theorem, Figure 2-7 is typically the kind of slide that you find, which is usually considered, at least by instructors, as acceptable.

Intercept Theorem : If you have a triangle *ABC*, and two points *D* and *E* on lines (*AB*) and (*AC*) such as the (*DE*) line is parallel to the (*BC*) line.

Then :

$$\frac{AD}{AB} = \frac{AE}{AC} \quad \text{and} \quad \frac{AD}{AB} = \frac{DE}{BC}$$

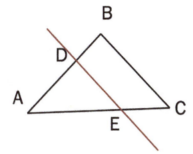

Figure 2-7. *The Intercept Theorem*

The amount of text isn't huge, besides it really is what you want students to note down and memorize. From a student perspective, if this arrives say after 35 minutes into a math class, odds are very high that presenting during class this slide or its Greek version will be very much the same.

Even if the quantity of information isn't frightening, it's nevertheless a mouthful and you may want, as in Figure 2-8, to take the original slide (on the left), and duplicate it (on the right) to introduce elements slowly. First the text that presents the context, then the triangle is shown, then the triggering event – the (DE) line - then the two ratio equalities that conclude the theorem. You have to be extremely willing to see here a Hollywood-type scenario, and it will probably escape students anyway. What the theorem lacks is a good story, and preferably a practical one. Fortunately, there is a story: it's said that the Greek mathematician Thales applied this theorem to measure the height of the pyramid of Cheops. There are some doubts about the authenticity of the story, but who cares? Legends are also stories.

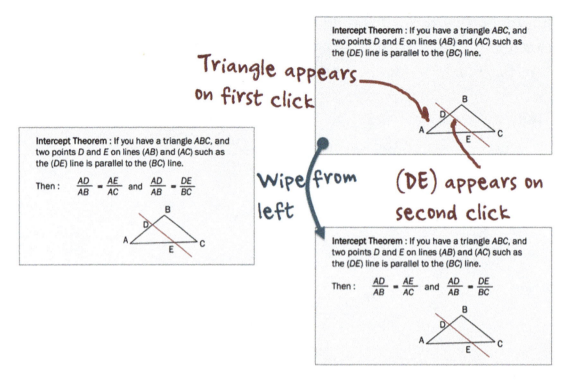

Figure 2-8. *Intercept Theorem, The Return*

I can add a schema illustrating this legend, as shown in Figure 2-9. One remark about the schema: I have tried to keep it as close as possible to a plain mathematical diagram. In particular, the schema seems to suggest that the extremity of the shadow of the stick should match the extremity of the shadow of the pyramid, which is of course no obligation. For simplicity, I have preferred to draw a single ray of sun, and not having to explain that as the sun is so far away, then all rays can be considered parallel in the neighborhood of the pyramid. No need to complicate the topic and mix physics with mathematics.

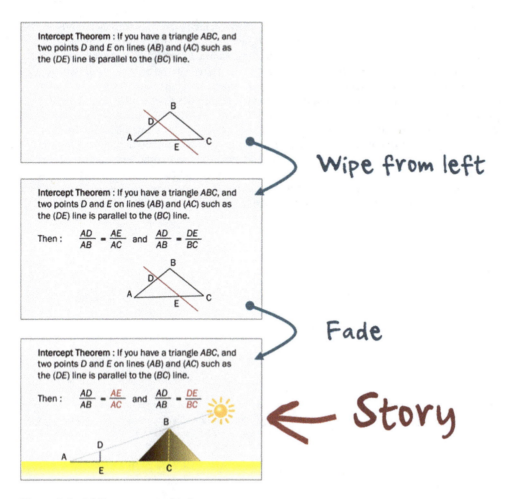

Figure 2-9. *Adding a story to the theorem*

Another point that is worth mentioning is that I've been working hard on continuity; I'm keeping the text of the theorem from the beginning to the end (which gives a chance to the audience for catching up) and I have placed my pyramid in such a way that its top coincides with the B tip of the triangle that it replaces; perhaps I could add that the pyramid is at a third of the slide, as was the original diagram. The shape of the pyramid is also relatively close to the triangle. Drawing the initial triangle exactly as the pyramid would probably have been a mistake, because in the pyramid schema the pyramid itself is not the triangle; the only tip that it shares with the original diagram is precisely the one that arrives at the same spot. The final diagram contains all the letters that are mentioned in the text of the theorem so that it can be related to the original diagram. In fact, the letters should probably appear separately after the slide is first shown.

If continuity provides the feeling that we are looking at a single unit when we seamlessly switch from one slide to the next, too much continuity may defeat our purpose. The story on the last slide, which should be a kind of climax, may look to the audience just like another boring mathematical diagram. There are some colors, and I have tried to keep the right balance between a mathematical diagram and a mildly realistic illustration, but I fear that it may not be enough to get people out of slumber. I need a visual break before my story.

The break that seems the best to me is a photograph, as shown in Figure 2-10. As with all famous landmarks, you can find as many pictures of the pyramids of Giza as you want; the only difficulty was finding a picture where a pyramid would fade naturally into the diagram. I have adjusted the picture so as to have the top of the middle pyramid to also match the B tip of the triangle in the previous slide, which still maintains continuity, together with the text of the theorem. A picture of Egyptian pyramids isn't what you would expect in a math class. The picture appearing after sober graphics should intrigue and rekindle interest, even in the middle of a class, especially as the link between the picture and the text of the theorem will only become apparent in the next slide. Continuity ensures that the flow is maintained. The diagram in the last slide may then be commented – and numerical values provided to your audience for computing the height of the pyramid. It makes for a far more attractive and, hopefully, memorable lesson than the original plain slide, still there in the series, but now part of a dynamic sequence of tightly knit slides. Time requirements to prepare this presentation aren't extremely high; in fact, what took me most time was finding a suitable picture that would integrate well with the other slides. Other than this, diagrams are easily drawn and animations quick to set in place.

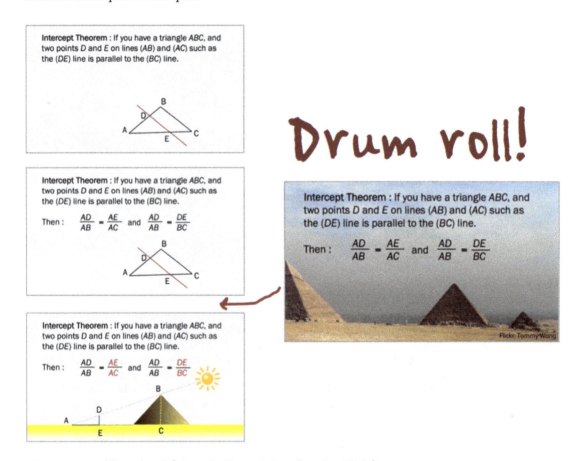

Figure 2-10. *Adding a break (picture by Tommy Wong, found on Flickr)*

The Human Factor

In retrospect, you may think that the example of the intercept theorem was a bit too easy; after all, there was a good, famous story. Now, what to do when there are no stories, no legends, nothing? Let's take for instance the Bolzano-Weierstrass theorem that says, as I am sure that you know:

A metrizable space is sequentially compact if and only if it is closed and bounded.

Bolzano-Weierstrass is to the intercept theorem what *Critique of the Pure Reason* is to *The Three Musketeers*.

If we have no story directly linked to the theorem, we still have Bernard Bolzano, and Karl Weierstrass; it's not really matter for a "Bolzano meets Weierstrass" Hollywood-style story – to start with they never met - but you can show them as in Figure 2-11 and a quick web search lets us tell some trivia about them. Whenever I mention someone, I try to show that someone. Not only theorems, but techniques, algorithms, everything is associated with people who first thought about it, and gave a form to their ideas; incidentally, I usually find those people far more interesting than those who populate tabloids. As human beings, we are wired to react to the faces of other human beings. Portraits wake up the audience, and give some warmth to what might be dry. Add one anecdote or two about the person you are showing, and you have an excellent break to reinvigorate a slumbering audience.

Bernard Bolzano
1781-1848

Karl Weierstrass
1815-1897

A metrizable space is sequentially compact if and only if it is closed and bounded.

Figure 2-11. *When there is no story, you still have people*

Portraits are very easy to find on the web. Even lesser-known figures can usually be found on specialized websites (on the history of mathematics, for instance). Today's people, as soon as they speak at conferences, can rather easily be found on Flickr or on their own site. There are very few people I couldn't find a representation of.

Thus, I see in a technical presentation stories not as the skeleton, but

- Either as the meat of the presentation when they illustrate an application of what is explained,

- Or as a way to get the audience out of lethargy by breaking the rhythm.

In the first case, if the point that is illustrated is an important one, the story should be preceded by a break. In the second case, the anecdote *is* the break, and a signal that you should pay attention. Anecdotes and stories greatly benefit from images, and portraits add a welcome human touch.

In all cases, the anecdotes double as mnemonics, associating an image with an idea.

Summary

In this chapter we covered the following:

- If building a technical presentation around a single story isn't always feasible, you can always think your presentation as a piece of music, first by establishing a continuity, then by raising interest through breaks surprising your audience.

- You can weave multiple stories in your score, and you can always find stories about the scientists and inventors who dreamt what you are talking of.

We are now going to see in detail the various elements we put on slides.

CHAPTER 3

■ ■ ■

Populating Slides

Dum taxat, rerum magnarum parva potest res exemplare dare et vestigia notitiai.

So far as it goes, a small thing may give analogy of great things, and show the tracks of knowledge.

—Lucretius (99 BC–55 BC)

I've talked about giving rhythm to slides; it's time to talk about what to put on them. There isn't much choice: either it will be text or graphical elements (I consider including a video as an aside, and not as really belonging to the presentation). If there is one certainty, it's that you should not display everything you have to say on your slides, especially all at once, because first, as a presenter, you are supposed to add value; and second, because your audience reads faster than you can speak.

Vision

For a long while, whenever I was reading "visionary" in the context of presentations – and some authors use the word a lot – it was conjuring in me images of those pioneers who understood very early the potential of new technologies and relentlessly, stubbornly developed what was to become major industries, when everybody was laughing at them: people like the Wright brothers, or Thomas Edison, or Henry Ford. As someone who was merely trying to explain to others how stuff works, with no ambition to become a beacon of light in an ocean of darkness, I wasn't considering myself a visionary.

I was wrong. Jonathan Swift wrote about vision that it's "the art of seeing what is invisible to others"; there is no specific reference to future in this definition; visionaries aren't limited to the narrow circle of great thinkers. We probably have all experienced the moment when, after trying for a long time to make sense of an obscure technical documentation, there was a sudden snap and everything fell in place. We could now picture what was so badly expressed in the docs, and understood it. This is vision, and this is what you want to share in a presentation. You cannot share experience otherwise than through stories that will make the talk more lively; by definition, experience takes time to acquire. There is no point in sharing precise details, which will soon be forgotten, or can better be found in a reference book or on the Web. You want to bring your audience to the point where, when they require some precise information, they will know exactly what to look for and be able to find it by themselves. You should put on your slides what you see, which your audience doesn't see yet: what even a demo cannot show. I've tried to illustrate allegorically in Figure 3-1 what "vision" means in a technical presentation context – nothing more than your understanding of how things work.

Figure 3-1. *The technical visionary (allegory), after Friedrich*

The vision you present doesn't need to be precise; it doesn't need to be accurate to the smallest detail. It needs to be the representation of a mental model – your mental model – what you see when you close your eyes. When I close my eyes, whatever I'm thinking of, I never see bullet points.

Text and Annotations

When you refer to "text" displayed during a presentation, you must differentiate between different types of text. There is informational text, which is what most people think about first and which can be described as comments on your topic; there is also text that *is* your topic, which I'll call *topic text*. Whenever I'm talking about programming, I have to display code. Technically speaking, it's text, but not the same type of text as the terrible (and real, although it's not a purely technical presentation) example in Figure 3-2.

Figure 3-2. *Just don't do it (picture by Daniel Latorre, found on Flickr)*

In Figure 3-2, the picture looks to be taken from the first ranks in what appears to be a large university auditorium. Binoculars were probably required from the top ranks. An experienced speaker, and this one isn't reading his slides, can still keep the audience interested. Simply, the slides are completely useless and add zero value. I cannot tell from the picture whether the text was displayed all at once, or if bullet points were displayed one by one, which would be a lesser evil. In any case, unless the speaker is an exceptional showman, you usually leave such a presentation with the feeling that you wouldn't have wasted all that time if a printout of the slides had simply been sent to you by email.

Obvious conclusion: there must be little informational text, which has two advantages:

- For people at the back of the room, you can use a far bigger font size.

- If you don't show much text, you have to limit yourself to what is important.

For me, the touchstone is what I would do (and it has happened to me a couple of times) if because of a technical glitch I had to manage without PowerPoint and only had a blackboard and a piece of chalk for tools - what I'd write on the blackboard is what I'll put on my slides.

The bad news: if you are supposed to hand out a document, you won't get rid of it by printing the slides; you'll have to work a little. The silver lining is that instead of having a set of slides that will be both poor presentation visuals and a hardly legible document, you will be able to provide, after a good presentation, a robust document. I have experimented with documents, I have a few ideas about them, and I'll come back to this topic later.

The case is different with text that truly belongs to your topic. If you need to comment a program, or a diagram, or prove a theorem, or explain a chemical reaction, you'll have to show what you are going to talk about. In my case, it's usually computer programs. A program can be quite a lot of text, with many issues linked to the layout and continuity between successive parts. Just like informational text, topic text should not be displayed all at once, but by small chunks. One simple way of achieving this result, illustrated in Figure 3-3, is to apply the same mechanism I have applied at the beginning of Chapter 2 with the three shapes:

- I first paste the text as a single piece on one slide. I usually color the code in the same way that a syntax-aware text editor does it.

- Then I duplicate the slide as many times as required, and, working back from the last slide to be shown in the series (the only slide that remains complete), I remove in every previous slide all the text that belongs to a chunk that will appear later. The arrows in Figure 3-3 indicate how I'm working back.

- Slides are displayed in the order indicated by the numbers in Figure 3-3.

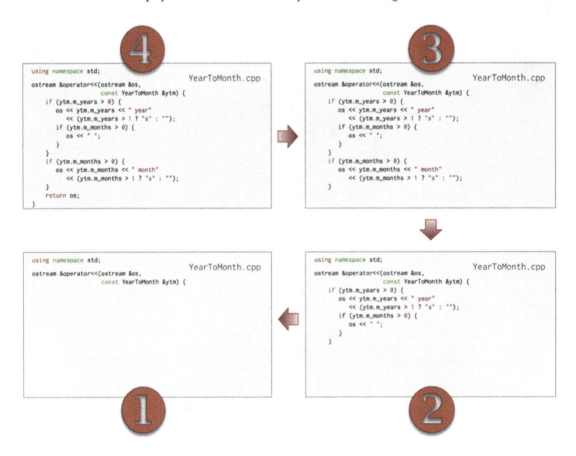

Figure 3-3. *Breaking topic text into smaller chunks*

There are more sophisticated ways, which we'll see later, of handling the different pieces, but this is a good way to obtain a satisfactory result without much effort or time investment.

The last type of text that I add to my slides, and which is for me significantly different from informational text and topic text, is annotation. I have started using annotations following an unhappy experience. I had to speak in California, and it was one of my first conferences outside Europe. To look more professional, I bought just before my trip a tiny laser pointer. During my talk, I wished to use it and underline an important point. I was rather far away from the screen, something like 10 to 12 feet; I had a dreadful stage fright – nine hours of jet lag to overcome (I had arrived from Paris the day before); and when I tried to underline the important point I was shaking so much that the little red dot was moving around like a crazy fly. I quickly turned off the pointer, hoping that not too many people noticed, and for easily ten years I never used this kind of tool again.

The lesson for me was that in difficult circumstances everything must be carefully prepared, and as easy to perform as possible. My must-have accessory, today, is a remote control, and the only button I press is "next slide." It includes a laser pointer, but I only use it when I feel inspired.

When I want to underline something, I prepare it beforehand, and you have an example in Figure 3-4. I write just a few words in a mock handwritten font (as I have said in Chapter 1, I use most often a font called *Ampersand*, but there are many to choose from). I sometimes slightly rotate the text, to give the feeling of something hastily scribbled. I don't hesitate to use colloquial or even slang words, to the contrary of regular text, which is usually rather formal. More often than not, I accompany my annotation with a hand-drawn arrow, which I draw with the PowerPoint scribble option (that's under "Shape," then under "Lines and Connectors").

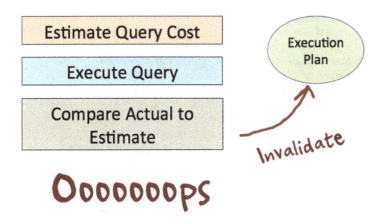

Figure 3-4. *Using annotations*

When the annotation appears, I start by animating the arrow if there is one (I'll dedicate a full chapter to animation) with a "wipe" animation from tail to head, trying to choose a wiping direction that matches the position of the arrow, and I apply the same "wipe" movement to the annotation, in the writing direction.

With experience, I discovered that this method has many benefits. First of all, it gives a feeling of spontaneity to something that has been carefully prepared. Another important benefit, to the contrary of a laser pointer even held steadily, the annotation remains until you click to make it disappear or move to the next slide. Someone who was shortly distracted will easily catch up and won't need to ask around what you are referring to, exactly.

Finally, it works very well in a video, and I find it far less coldly technical than the large yellow spot that some people use to focus attention; the annotation has the human touch.

Here is the rule for text: only important points or what you need to comment, plus annotations that punctuate the speech. Limiting oneself to text, though, is very frugal, and very often you'll want to add graphical elements to your slides.

Graphical Elements

As I said at the beginning of this chapter, a technical presentation is for me projecting my own vision, and my vision isn't text only. In fact, my vision isn't much text. There are roughly four possibilities for adding graphical elements in presentation software such as PowerPoint:

- Regular charts, bar charts, and all their relatives;
- What is called "SmartArt";
- Pictures;
- And finally shapes.

Charts and SmartArt

I use charts very rarely because, as I have previously said, I like to make elements pop up as I am ready to comment them. A chart in PowerPoint is a single object; you can sometimes cheat and try not to show everything at once, but options are extremely limited. There is often a lot of information in a chart. If I want to explore it in detail, or if I simply want more flexibility, I usually prefer re-creating a chart with shapes, which I'll discuss when I talk about shapes later in this chapter.

If I don't like charts much, my feelings for them are very warm compared to those I have for "SmartArt"; I find SmartArt rather static (even if contrary to charts there are options for making the figures appear not as a single object but little by little, which is great), and I feel extremely uncomfortable with what I tend to regard as freeze-dried instant thinking. Figure 3-5 tries to express my feelings about SmartArt. Anybody who hasn't just graduated has already seen these graphics umpteen times, in presentations, on websites, in glossy brochures, in white papers. After a while, people don't really remember what was written in these circles the last time – was it "Action Plan, Strategy, Mission, Vision"? "Data Collection, Analysis, Tuning"? "Eeeny, Meeny, Miny, Moe"? These graphics aren't intrinsically bad; they give a pleasant feeling of clarity, of organized thinking, and of strategic vision. The problem is that I suspect that your audience will forget about them as soon as the presentation is over, because they have seen these graphics far too many times already. To be complete, on Windows you can "ungroup," which means breaking into its component parts, a SmartArt figure (I'm talking about grouping at the end of this chapter), and on Mac you can select pieces individually and change them, so you don't need to stick with default graphics and can bring a light touch of originality.

Figure 3-5. *SmartArt, the dinner helper of uninspired presentations (allegory)*

Nevertheless, instead of enhancing the message , SmartArt may in some instances dumb it down; some kind of diagram with three circles respectively inscribed with "Blood," "Sweat," and "Tears" lacks impact for me. I am touching here what will be, I fear, a recurrent theme in this chapter: if you want the graphical element to enrich, rather than decorate, your message; if you want it to stick into the minds and remain attached as a mnemonic to what you want to transmit, the graphical element must be new; or the association must be unusual. To the contrary, attaching your message to cliché makes it instantly unremarkable.

Now, remember that the purpose of your visuals is to transmit your vision to your audience. If a SmartArt graphic exactly matches your mental model, by all means use it; it's not because it doesn't belong to my mental universe that it shouldn't belong to yours. However, if your purpose is simply to make a plain list look better, you'd probably rather abstain.

What I use in my presentations is almost exclusively pictures and shapes, sometimes combined.

Pictures

Let's start with pictures. For PowerPoint, they are either "cliparts" or images that you read from a file. Most presentation specialists agree: if you want to look like a pro, avoid cliparts, and use "stock photography," photographs taken by professionals, which you can buy from agencies.

I won't quite follow the flow. What is wrong with cliparts? Cliparts are these little images that are provided with your presentation software and are supposed to illustrate simple concepts. The big issue with standard cliparts, and by standard cliparts I mean cliparts that you can browse in your presentation software, is that for one concept, there aren't many suitable images inside the library. There is often only one. The result, when a speaker wants to illustrate the "idea" concept, he or she will use a light bulb. To mean "international," what is better than an earth globe? - and to talk about strategy, a compass is perfect; and for an agreement, shaking hands. Obviously, there are kinds of presentations in which these are frequent concepts. This causes, after a few presentations, a very strong feeling of déjà vu: exactly as with SmartArt. Your message will be lost in the crowd of messages that used similar representations.

The problem with cliparts is not the clipart: the problem is cliché. Generally speaking, trying to express an abstract idea with a clipart is prone to cliché; however, cliparts are quite useful for representing information technology hardware, for instance, or icons commonly used in programs. Additionally, cliparts are very easy to combine with shapes.

The sites I usually visit for cliparts are openclipart.org and wpclipart.com. Both store tens of thousands of public domain illustrations.

The greatest difficulty when using cliparts is to maintain style consistency throughout your presentation; you cannot use a cartoon-like clipart alongside a photographic clipart (the examples in Figure 3-6 are pretty discordant). The openclipart.org website gives the name of the author (or uploader) and allows you to browse collections by author. Once you have selected one clipart that really suits your needs, try to check the production of the same author; using the production of one or few authors will give your presentation a better consistency.

Figure 3-6. *What is wrong with clipart*

On the cliché rating scale, stock photography fares rather poorly. Stock photography is what you find on all corporate websites, pictures of dark-suited models pretending to be young dynamic executives as the samples in Figure 3-7. Or in these group pictures you find in the brochures of training companies, attendees happily gathered around a computer screen and looking relaxed, with toothpaste-ad smiles, all young (except the middle-aged instructor, who must be credibly experienced), all better looking than average, with a careful gender and ethnicity balance. When I'm done with my trainees and students, they look rather tired. Me too, probably.

Figure 3-7. *What is wrong with stock photography (pictures by Adam Grabek, thetaxheaven and Steve Wilson, found on Flickr)*

We have all seen these technically impeccable pictures everywhere, and so has your audience. If you want to be memorable, be different, I believe that technical presentations are presentations where you can be slightly offbeat.

For photographs, and sometimes engravings or paintings, I mostly have two sources:

- Flickr – you may have noticed it already - where I stick to what is free for commercial use and free to modify (you can select by license – I give in Appendix B a quick overview of image licensing). There are fantastic Creative Commons pictures on Flickr, including stock-photography type as in Figure 3-7. What I'm looking for, though, is usually candid pictures with real people who don't look like they are coming straight from a magazine ad.

- My second main source, which I mostly use for portraits of famous people, is Wikimedia Commons.

Why do we want images in a technical presentation? There are several reasons. You may want to represent what you are talking of, a pure illustration. For instance, when teaching programming, the first class is usually devoted to a short history of computers. An important milestone was the *pascaline*, Blaise Pascal's mechanical calculator that he invented when he was 19, around the mid-17th century. A few of these machines still survive, and I usually want to show one (you'll see it in the next chapter). A portrait is also an illustration (Blaise Pascal will appear in the next chapter too).

Not far from illustrations, there are images that I would call evocative or contextual. These pictures are very useful for breaks. You have seen an example of a contextual image in Chapter 2: the picture of the pyramids in Giza was used for a break but also had the purpose of defining the context for an application of the intercept theorem. Contextual images can also show analogies, or simply be images that come to your mind to illustrate, possibly with a smile, a slightly abstract concept. I've shown in Figure 3-8 different possible ways of introducing a concept that I often have to mention whenever I talk about database performance, waits in the system. Even if waits are very real, you cannot show a wait, you can only evoke the idea. One way to evoke waits is to use, as shown in the smaller top slide in Figure 3-8, this well-known symbol for a computer that isn't responsive: an hourglass.

Figure 3-8. *Contextual images (pictures by, clockwise, Richard-G, Tripp, Adam Harvey, and Deng Xiaojun, found on Flickr)*

If the hourglass is an immediately identifiable symbol, it's also a worn-out symbol; it's cliché. The four other slides in Figure 3-8 are photographs I have found in the Creative Commons section of Flickr by looking for the keyword "wait," as well as trying some related expressions such as "waiting line" or "queue." These are just a few examples that I picked among dozens of candidates. All of them are more attractive and more memorable than the hourglass. I might use any one depending on my state of mind, how well the photograph matches my current palette (don't neglect this aspect), and my audience; people waiting for an underground train will resonate better with an audience living in a metropolis and using public transport than with an audience from a small city using their own cars.

Finally, I also use images for breaks that aren't immediately relevant to what I'm talking about. I often use images to express my personal mood or what I assume my audience feels (which is a way to manifest empathy). Here again you can easily get a few smiles, especially when you hit the nail on the head. Figure 3-9 illustrates a number of these empathy pictures that bring some relief when the going gets tough (I usually put them over or next to those puzzling things I'm trying to explain). I use pictures of children, like the one at the bottom of Figure 3-9, pretty regularly. Children are often awfully expressive, and there are no cultural barriers with this kind of picture (which isn't the case with gestures, as some innocent gesture in one country can be extremely rude in another one). I have processed all these photographs, and removed the backgrounds; I'll explain how in the next chapter.

Figure 3-9. *Empathy images (pictures by, top to bottom, Paul Downey, Incase, Orin Zebest, David Long, and Upsilon Andromedae, found on Flickr)*

When the picture is supposed to express your feelings, rather than those of the audience, you can even use an image that contradicts what you say; your audience will believe the image, not your words.

Other images useful for breaks are portraits of people that you quote. Quote slides, which Garr Reynolds likes very much, are a good way to add a break, and to make people smile and think. Over time, I built a collection of currently more than fifty images showing people I like to quote, or whom I could quote. I add to the portrait, for a more personal touch, the signature, which you can usually find for most famous dead people who lived in the past 500 years. I scale the images to a 1024 by 768 pixels size, which corresponds to the 4:3 slide format I use most often, and save them as JPEG files. Figure 3-10 shows a few samples from my collection (I never hesitate to quote people who are long dead about today's technologies; it's also part of the surprise element that wakes up the audience).

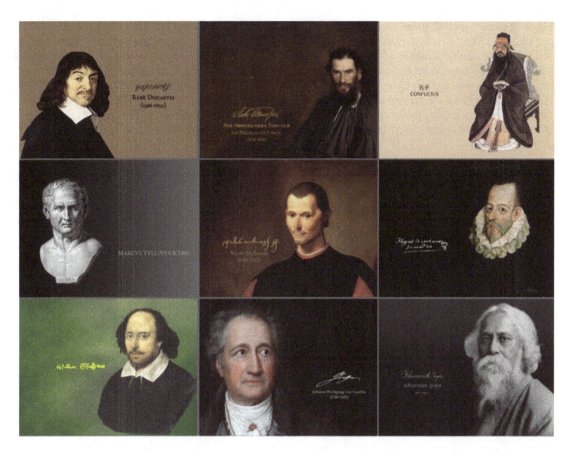

Figure 3-10. *Sample quote slides*

An image thus prepared can be used as a slide background. My quote images allow me to add the quote as a text box and change it at will. I often try to use a character font that evokes the period when the quote author was alive.

There is finally a last type of image other than clipart or picture: screenshots. I will elaborate on this topic (and give examples) in later chapters, but some advanced PowerPoint operations are more easily performed with images than with text or the shapes that we are going to see next. A screenshot of a slide is an easy way to turn into an image whatever you want on a slide. In the particular case of a software-related presentation, screenshots are also extremely useful for sketching the user interface, as discussed in the next section.

Shapes

Other than pictures, the graphical elements I use most are shapes. Technical presentations are often schema heavy, far more than business presentations. Because scientific and engineering talks are mostly about phenomena you cannot demonstrate during a presentation, they rely a lot on diagrams. In the academic world, "instructor resources" that accompany a textbook are usually at least composed of figures from the text for inclusion in slides.

Interestingly we have with diagrams as many issues, if not more, as with text. Let's take a look at the diagram in Figure 3-11, found on Wikimedia, which explains the important problem of waste in nuclear plants. It's a very good diagram, far better than the average. It's clear, pleasant to look at, and nevertheless this diagram suffers exactly the same deficiencies as a text-heavy slide: it contains a lot of information that your audience cannot absorb all at once, and the text is far too small to be read from afar (the size of the text in the yellow rectangles with rounded corners is around 8 when the diagram extends from top to bottom as shown). People in the first ranks, if they have the sight of a jet-fighter pilot, will read everything quickly then check email on their smartphones, which people in the last ranks will already be doing. Additionally, the format of this diagram indicates that it was thought for a document page, not a slide; it makes the layout awkward. The colors were selected with taste but they may not match your palette.

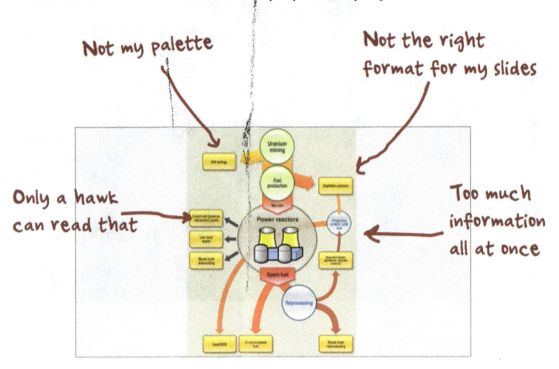

Figure 3-11. *Diagram issues*

I re-create this type of diagram with shapes. Shape formatting is often tedious (format options are available by right-clicking on the selected shape), but by copying and pasting the amount of time required to completely redo even a complex diagram isn't tremendous. I have done it with the nuclear waste diagram using my Apress palette from Chapter 1; and the result, which at first sight looks much worse than the original diagram, is shown in Figure 3-12.

The slide looks far busier than the original diagram, because I have tried to make every piece of text as big as possible (the size of text in the rectangles with rounded corners is now 20 in most of them, and 18 where there is a lot of text or long words). Even if the schema isn't as aesthetically pleasing as the original one, it matches the palette, it matches the slide format, and most important it remains legible from the back of the room. It only contains shapes, one clipart (found on `www.openclipart.org`), and three text boxes. The reason for using text boxes is that, although you can add text to any shape (right-click on a selected shape to see "Format Text"), the text added to a shape is always centered within the shape. I didn't want "New Fuel" or "Power reactors" to be centered, and I wanted "Spent Fuel" to appear horizontally over a tilted arrow. Overlaying text boxes did the job.

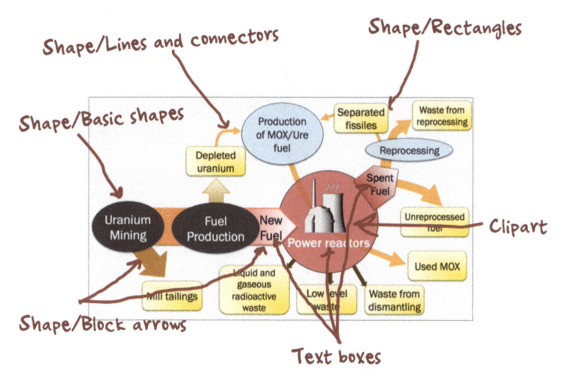

Figure 3-12. *Redrawing a diagram with shapes (and a clipart)*

Other than flexibility over color, size, and layout, the real advantage of re-creating diagrams with shapes is the ability, as every element in the diagram is now an independent object, to apply exactly the same method I have applied with code in Figure 3-3 and copy the slide a number of times, then remove shapes from the slide before the last and process backwards, so that when slides are shown the full diagram appears piece after piece. Breaking the diagram over multiple slides is illustrated in Figure 3-13.

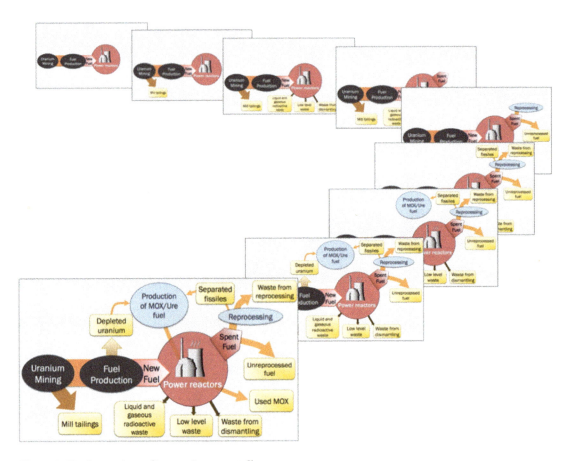

Figure 3-13. *Presenting a diagram incrementally*

The last slide is exactly the same one as in Figure 3-12, but because you made the whole schema appear bit by bit the subjective feeling will no longer be the same sentiment of being overwhelmed with information. It would also be possible to change the colors of previously commented elements on the slide (giving them some degree of transparency, or desaturating the colors, which means making them grayer) so as to focus on each element in turn. Additionally, I would probably use animations, which I'll discuss in Chapter 6.

As I said earlier in this chapter, I usually also re-create charts with shapes. Bar charts are just two lines for the axes, rectangles, and text for labels. For pie charts, there is a shape conveniently named "pie" that you can adjust to get the angle you want. Insert the chart you want to reproduce into your slide, draw your shapes over it, and then remove the original chart when you are done. You are ready to go, you can animate everything the way you want, and have a dynamic chart.

Shapes have many other uses. I use them for highlighting, nothing more than a yellow rectangle placed at the background; and for annotations, especially arrows that are hand drawn with the "scribble" line shape, and completed with a handwritten font.

What I really like shapes for, however, is as building blocks for a kind of stage set, to sketch a user interface. Let me explain my thoughts with first a simple example.

Web searches have become a regular fixture of our lives. You may need to show a web search in one of your presentations. What are your options?

- The live demo: exiting the presentation software, opening a browser, and searching.

- Inserting screenshots of an actual search in your slides.

- Faking it.

Whenever I can, I try to keep live demos separate from presentations. Interrupting a slideshow, starting something else, and trying to resume the slideshow where you left is disturbing both for the audience and for the presenter. Additionally, you'd better prepare beforehand a browser window with the proper URL, and zooming should be adjusted to make the window a comfortable reading for the folks in the last rank. The problem with live search demos is uncertainty. They offer ample opportunities for typos, possibly with embarrassing auto-completion and, especially if you are presenting in a foreign country, search results may differ sensibly from what you were expecting. In a sales-related presentation, how will your audience react if all of a sudden the name of your biggest competitor pops up as a "sponsored search result"?

Using screenshots of the search (or embedding a video recording) eliminates uncertainty, typos, and embarrassment from the equation. You still have the problem of magnifying the page to make it legible, but this is workable. A few issues remain, though. The results of the search may in some cases date it; you may not want anybody to notice that you first prepared your presentation three years ago. Searches often return irrelevant results that may be a distraction for some. Finally, you'll have to choose one search engine, and strangely this seemingly innocuous choice may alienate a part of your audience (I wouldn't use Bing at a Linux conference).

This is why I prefer the third option, "faking it," which I do with shapes. I'm not interested in the search engine but in the "Web search" concept, and all I need to do is "sketch" it, as illustrated in Figure 3-14. I only need two shapes: a white rectangle that will be my search field, to which I'll add a dark gray border and an inner shade; and another rectangle that contains "Search," which will be gray, with a little 3D effect, and which will simulate a button. My cursor is an oversized cursor image that even people at the back of the room will see easily. With a touch of animation, it will be a perfectly decent search page, which will be followed by a slide that shows what I want my audience to see.

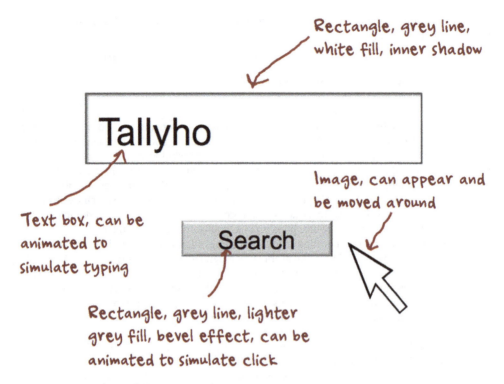

Figure 3-14. *Web search in a presentation*

A search page is a simple example; but you can sketch far more complicated user interfaces with shapes. You can use these sketches for mock demos or, once you have explained your vision and principles, for showing how to perform a particular operation.

For instance, what about explaining how to use PowerPoint-like presentation software? You can do it for real, or you can use a sketch to focus very precisely on the steps to perform. Sketching presentation software with shapes is easy, and you can see the result in Figure 3-15. I have modeled my generic presentation-software window after PowerPoint, but the sketch would look familiar enough to the user of any version of any presentation software: nothing else than carefully aligned rectangles. The window is a rectangle, the ribbon menu at the top, which doesn't interest me as long as I don't need to talk about anything particular on it, is a rectangle; slides are rectangles, I have added a shadow to my slide rectangles; and on the left-hand side I have changed the color of the line around one slide to make it the current slide. My stage set is ready. I have added my cursor image (which can be as big as I want, as it's just a plain image).

Figure 3-15. *Sketching presentation software*

I can use the slide represented in Figure 3-15 for showing a lot of different features, and even showing operations I couldn't in a real demo. Let's take a precise example: I want to show how to format a shape. It requires selecting a shape; you need to left-click on your mouse, and people cannot see it in a demo, you can only tell them. Then, same story with the right-click required to make the contextual menu appear. What cannot be shown in a demo can be shown in a presentation, simply by adding mouse cliparts with an emphasis on the correct button as shown in Figure 3-16.

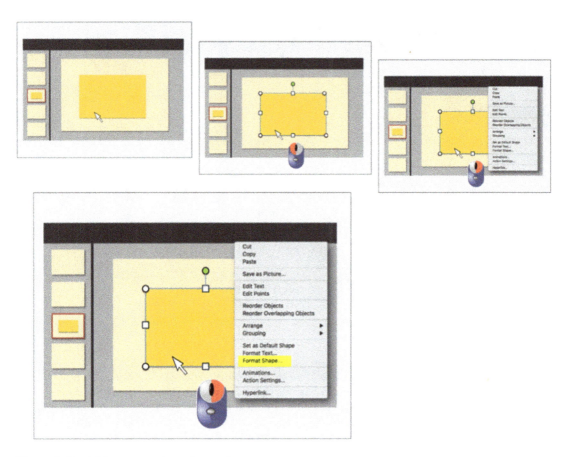

Figure 3-16. *A fake presentation software demo*

I have also added a real PowerPoint screenshot – but nothing more than the menu that opens when I right-click. I have edited the screenshot of a full PowerPoint window to only keep this menu (image editing is the topic of the next chapter), and I have actually slightly modified the image (for instance, as the screenshot was taken on a Mac, I have erased keyboard shortcuts that are too specific and might disturb a Windows or Linux user). As this menu is an image, I can give it the size I want in exactly the same way as I can with the mouse pointer. To indicate that the yellow rectangle is selected, I have added to it a blue border, small discs at the corners (plus a green one above, the rotation handler), and small squares in the middle of each sides; but all these elements are shapes and I made them far more visible than they would be for real. There is a theatrical quality to a fake demo composed of shapes, cliparts, and parts of screenshots. Victor Hugo once wrote that theater is not the land of reality, but the land of truth, and in the same way a fake demo may not be an exact representation of reality, but far more understandable and in a way "truer" than plain reality.

There is for this kind of presentation a higher initial amount of work than when you just show to the audience the screen of your laptop and start opening windows and really running software. By happily duplicating slides, copying, and pasting, the total amount of work required is in fact not as high as it may look. In any case, such a type of presentation allows you to show what you could only talk about with a real demo (mouse clicks, finger swipes) and to really put the focus where you want it to be; but, it's important, it also allows you to concentrate on what you say rather than what you do. Having only to click on "next slide," you can look at your audience and better interact with it, which is invaluable.

Layers and Groups

Before concluding this chapter, I'd like to talk about layers and groups of objects. Whenever you insert a new object on a slide, whether this object is a textbox or an image, it's stacked above the previous objects in a plane of its own. You can imagine the slide as a stack of transparent layers, each one containing one object. If you select the object and right-click, the contextual menu shows an "Arrange" submenu (you can see it in Figure 3-16) in which you find the following choices:

- Bringing the object to the top of the stack (*Bring to Front*),

- Sending it to the bottom of the stack (*Send to Back*),

- Or exchanging its plane with the plane of the object that is either just above or just below it (*Bring Forward/Send Backward*).

Some versions of PowerPoint allow to drag and drop planes in a 3D representation, but the options listed above are available everywhere. If you check the biggest (and last) slide in Figure 3-16, you can see that I have highlighted "Format Shape" in the contextual menu with a yellow rectangle: this rectangle is placed *below* the menu. When I processed the menu image, I made its background transparent: the gray background that you see is actually a separate, plain gray image under the text. The yellow rectangle is placed between those two layers. Planes are extremely important when you start animating objects as we'll do in Chapter 6, because an object always moves within its own plane. When another object is placed in its path, if the moving object is supposed to appear before the other object, it must absolutely be placed higher in the stack, and vice versa.

The "Grouping" menu below "Arrange" also allows you, if you have selected several objects, to group them together (you may sometimes find grouping and ungrouping operations as choices under an "Arrange" menu, next to stack displacement operations). Objects that are grouped become a compound object that can be dragged around (and animated) as if it were a single object, and all the components of the compound object are brought into a single layer.

Selecting many objects is sometimes tedious, especially when they are small and close to each other, or when they overlap. When you want to group a very large number of objects together, it's often more convenient to duplicate the slide, remove everything that won't belong to the group, and go to the "Edit" menu and click on "Select All." Then you can group, copy the compound object, and paste it back in place.

I can illustrate layers and grouping with a representation I regularly use whenever I teach programming (in any computer language). I like to follow a program step by step and show what is really happening in memory through graphical representations. In particular, when you handle values in a program, they are stored at very precise locations in memory to which you give a name in your program and that are known as *variables*, meaning that the value stored can change. When I explain this, I draw my variables as boxes, in which I'll store values. Figure 3-17 shows one such box, created with simple shapes.

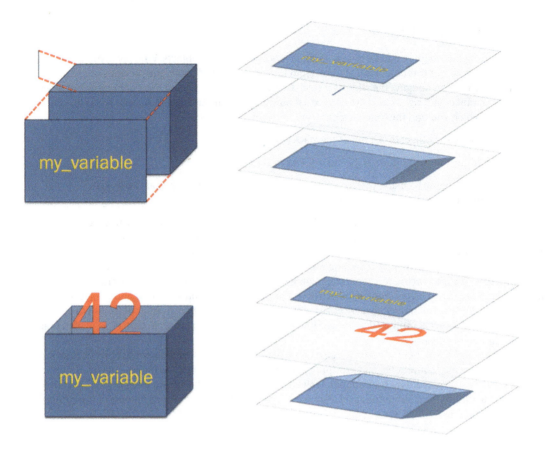

Figure 3-17. *Practical application of shapes, layers and grouping*

In the top-left corner of Figure 3-17 you can see how I create my box out of three different shapes: I start from the standard cube shape (cuboid would be more accurate than cube). As I want something that doesn't look like a solid brick but as an empty box, I'm adding a short vertical line segment that extends from the upper-left corner of the shape down to the horizontal line that represents the top edge of the front face; this segment of line simulates an inside edge. I cannot stop there, because if I want to show storing values *inside* the box (an operation known as an "assignment" in programming), I must be able to insert the layer containing the value between a box background and a box foreground. My box foreground is a simple rectangle that has exactly the same size as the front side of the brick, overlaid on it, and inscribed with the name of the variable (as the text is linked to the rectangle, it belongs to the same layer; a text box laid over the rectangle would be an independent layer). I end up with the three layers that you see at the top right of Figure 3-17. As the little line segment has no reason to live independently from the box background (I won't want to move it alone, nor to insert layers between this segment and the background), I group it with the background, merging in effect the two layers into one as you can see at the bottom right of Figure 3-17. I can then insert a layer with the value I want to store in my box, which really looks inside it and not merely above it. With animation, the effect is even more striking.

Thinking with layers is something that is useful in presentation software, and also when editing images as you'll see in the next chapter.

Summary

In this chapter we covered the following:

- Presenting a technical topic is mostly presenting your own vision of it, and this vision isn't so much text, unless some kind of text such as computer code is the topic of your talk, rather than images; or mostly shapes and cliparts for diagrams.

- Shapes are great for sketching a user interface.

- Every element in a slide belongs to a layer, and they can be grouped.

It's rare to find images that exactly match what you want to show, and that fit exactly with the general style of your presentation. We are going to see in the next chapter how to use images and how to edit them.

CHAPTER 4

■ ■ ■

Editing Images

What we hope ever to do with ease, we must learn first to do with diligence.

—Samuel Johnson (1709-1784)

I've talked in the previous chapter about images, and about where to find them. Unfortunately, if finding a good image is relatively easy, you usually need to modify and edit it; editing can be very simple or can require a significant amount of work. Before I start, I remind you that images, unless they are in the public domain, are subject to licensing terms allowing you, or not, to modify them, and allowing you, or not, to use them in a commercial context. All images used in this chapter are either in the public domain or Creative Commons images that are free to modify and use in a commercial context.

I'll illustrate editing in this chapter with an example I mentioned in the previous one: presenting in the course of a history of computing Blaise Pascal's mid-17th-century calculator (also known as a *Pascaline*, pronounced *Pasca-leen*). I'll be dealing with very common practical issues, which will allow you to learn the basics.

Placing Images on a Slide

When it comes to putting illustrative images on a slide, many people just do that: they put an illustrative image somewhere on the slide, as shown at the top of Figure 4-1. Most people have an innate feeling that putting it straight in the middle doesn't look right, and will instinctively put it on a third (a line of strength) or, even better, at the intersection of two lines of strength. Such a vignette, though, lacks impact and somehow the picture appears as a foreign element that doesn't blend too well into the slide.

Edge to Edge

You can contrast the top slide with the bottom slide in the figure, where I have simply increased the size of the picture so as to cover the full surface of the slide, and overlaid the year, the caption, and the image credits on it. Resizing the image is also an excellent opportunity for reframing it: pictures of museum exhibits such as 17th-century mechanical calculators are taken in showcases (unless they were taken by a professional photographer accredited with the museum). It's almost impossible for the photographer to frame as closely as he or she would when taking the picture, even with a zoom lens, and very hard to limit reflections and glares. There is at the bottom of the original picture a fragment of a purple label (not too visible in Figure 4-1), which can be eliminated by reframing, which you simply do by extending the picture *outside* the slide area so as to only keep the interesting bits over the surface of the slide. When the photograph is reframed, you'll probably want to make it match the size of the slide: by right-clicking on the image and selecting "Format Picture," you have options to crop it. The interesting area in the window is "Crop position" in the bottom half. If "Left" or "Top," or both, contains a negative value, set it to zero; the negative value just means that the upper-left corner of the picture is currently outside the slide, setting the value to zero states that you want the new official upper-left corner of the photograph to coincide with the upper-left corner of the slide.

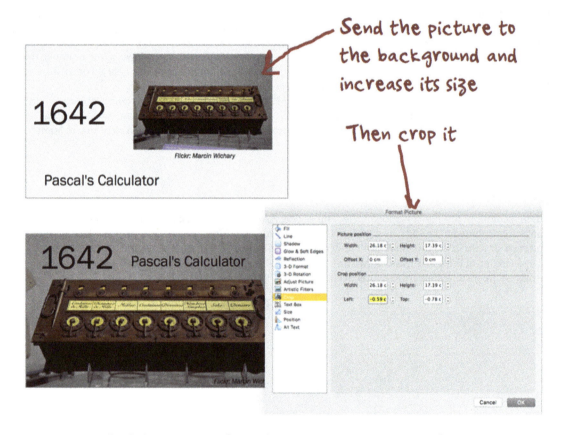

Figure 4-1. *Pascal's calculator, raw image (picture by Marcin Wichary, found on Flickr)*

Then lower down the values in "Width" and "Height" until the image covers exactly the size of the slide (in case of doubt, it's better if the image spills over a little – a narrow light line on the edge, corresponding to an incompletely covered background, looks ugly).

In the example the light background is perfect for displaying text. If you can find an area in the picture that is in a uniform color and large enough to accommodate whichever text you need to display, you have nothing more to do than select a font color that contrasts well with the background. Sometimes, however, the photograph is a mix of lights and shades, and if a part of your text is perfectly visible, another part of it fades helplessly in the background. I have illustrated this problem in Figure 4-2, with a photograph of a bust of Blaise Pascal, which I have actually modified to increase the contrast between the bust and its background. If I want to add text that overflows the width of the bust, as shown in the top two slides, either the middle or the extremities of the text suffers of poor contrast.

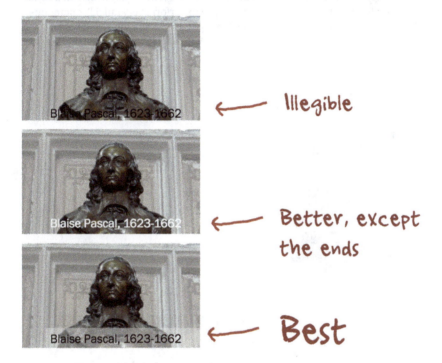

Figure 4-2. *Contrast issues with text (picture by Jebulon, found on Wikimedia Commons)*

The solution in that case is to right-click on the text box, select "Format Shape," and change the "Fill" color from "None" to something neutral (white or light gray are usually safe choices with a dark font color), and to set transparency around 50%. Your text will appear clearly, without being intrusive. I find that it works better if the semitransparent rectangle extends to one of the edges (which I have done in Figure 4-2); a semitransparent rectangle hanging in the middle of nowhere looks a bit strange to me.

Background Removal

The other option for blending the image into the slide (an option not exclusive of making the image bigger) is removing its background. The case for removing the background is particularly compelling with what I have called "empathy pictures" in the previous chapter – images that I use for a break and which I lay over what I'm talking about to express what the audience probably feels. Such a picture mustn't hide the topic of the presentation. Background removal also makes it easier to put the image across the edge of the slide. This is a technique I've learned from John McWade, the entirety of the image doesn't need to be *inside* the slide; a cropped image is often legible and "extends" the slide. You can remove the background with image editing software, and I'll devote a large part of this chapter to Gimp, the free image editing software I'm using.

There is, however, an easier way than manually erasing the background of an image. PowerPoint includes a rather impressive tool for performing this task, and it's shown in action in Figure 4-3. The "Format Picture" menu features a "Remove Background" button. Everything that will be made transparent is turned to a purplish color. You can first adjust a frame to surround what you want to keep, then you can click or draw lines in places that the tool wants to remove to indicate that you want to keep them (and vice versa). With the calculator picture, the tool wanted to remove the acrylic pieces supporting the device, thus creating splits into it, and I had to reintegrate them into the final image. This background removal tool works very well when what interests you strongly contrasts with its background (if you want to display a logo on a white background, for instance, the result is perfect); in that case it allows you to perform very quickly operations that are sometimes a bit tedious to perform otherwise. When the highlights or the shadows of the object blend into the background, or when the background isn't plain, the tool no longer works so well and you get far better results with techniques explained later in this chapter.

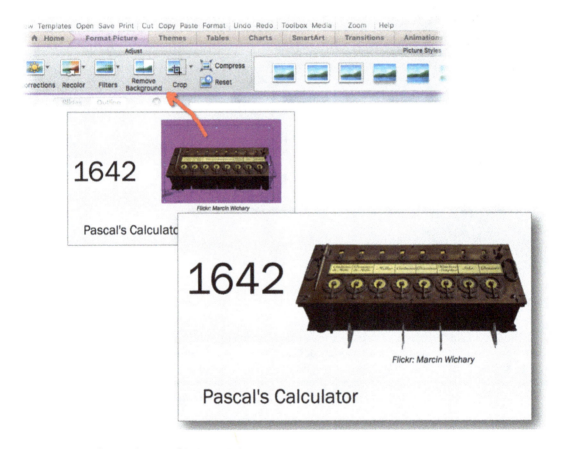

Figure 4-3. *Background removal in PowerPoint*

You may share my opinion that the acrylic support under the Pascaline is less noticeable in the context of the full showcase picture, where it makes sense, than when the background is removed. This might be a reason for looking for a different picture of another, support-less, calculator, and I found such a public domain image on Wikimedia Commons (https://commons.wikimedia.org/wiki/File:Pascalina.jpg). There is just one flaw with this picture of a different model of the calculator: its size is 300 by 197 pixels, and it's not available in a higher resolution.

Small Images

It happens from time to time that the best, or sometimes only, image that you find to illustrate a part of your talk is too small, either because the whole image was small, or because what interests you is actually a detail in a much bigger image. When I am confronted with such a case, I usually adopt one of two strategies: camouflage or flashiness.

Figure 4-4 illustrates camouflage. If you try to enlarge an image that is too small to make it go from edge to edge, pixels will show and the image will look very ragged from a short distance and very blurry from the back of the room. A slightly dishonest but effective way to make the image more palatable is to suggest that the lack of detail is an aesthetic choice rather than poor resolution.

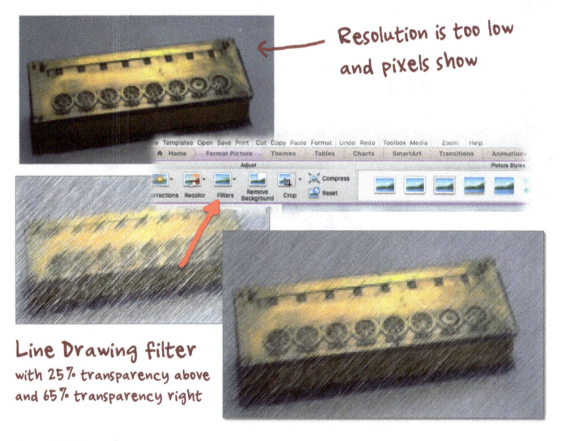

Figure 4-4. *Camouflage*

If you are using PowerPoint (if not, don't worry, you'll see soon ways of achieving similar or better results with Gimp), click the "Filter" button to the left of "Remove Background" (filters are also available in the "Format Image" menu when right-clicking on an image); in some versions of PowerPoint, filters are called "Artistic Effects."

There are many effects available, not all of them quite convincing in my opinion. To see their names you need to hover over icons. The filter that best suits my own tastes is the one called "Line Drawing," which you see applied in Figure 4-4 (I might be tempted in some cases by "Pastels Smooth"). All filters can be adjusted; one of the options is a transparency percentage. The default transparency level is 25%, where you start to wonder why you bothered to look for an actual picture of Pascal's calculator instead of showing a shoebox. Setting the transparency level at 65% makes the image relatively visible, while completely hiding the pixels, even when projected on a large screen.

The opposite tactic, flashiness, consists in keeping the image small – and to fly high the flag of smallness. Figure 4-5 shows the two different approaches to presenting a low-resolution image when nothing better is available. Instead of keeping it as an ill-fitted vignette as in the slide at the top of Figure 4-1, I'll use the image formatting options to turn it into a mock paper photograph, with a narrow white border and a shadow, and I tilt it very slightly to give the feeling of having dropped it here carelessly.

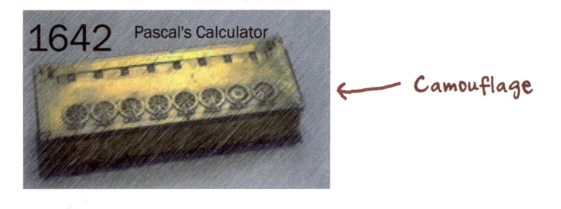

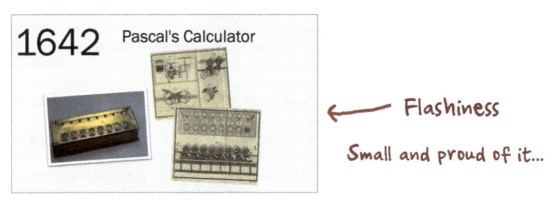

Figure 4-5. *Two ways of dealing with a low-resolution image*

I have joined to the small photograph two old engravings showing the internal mechanism, which I have kept small as well. I feel that keeping an image small works better when you can display several related images at once – it gives a feeling that you kept the picture small to show more (the real reason is of course that you kept it small because it was ugly when enlarged). Using several small pictures also works well, even if resolution is high enough, when you have at your disposal a few correct pictures but none of a quality that bears gracefully enough the edge-to-edge treatment.

The transformations that have been presented so far are simple, and can be performed in a matter of seconds without quitting PowerPoint. If you are using other presentation software, or if your images are such that the limits of easy tools are reached, then you need to use actual image editing software. I use Gimp (which stands for *GNU Image Manipulation Program*), an excellent product that perfectly suits my needs, with two great characteristics:

- It's free;

- It's available on Windows, Linux, and Mac (I've personally been using it in all three environments).

A Gimp Crash Course

There are many (thick) books on Gimp, and I certainly don't plan to explain to you every feature of it. For a start, I'm far from having used every feature, and the set I use is rather limited. I'll try in the remainder of this chapter to show you how you can use Gimp (or any similar program) to apply to images transformations that can make them more suitable for a presentation. The operations I have previously shown with PowerPoint can all be performed with Gimp, which you may find useful if you aren't using PowerPoint, or an older version. Gimp can also go where PowerPoint doesn't venture.

Before I start, I must give you a bit of background on images in general and Gimp.

What You Must Know

Image formats are very numerous. Gimp can open an image in almost any format and save it in almost any format. In practice, we have to deal with four formats:

- .jpg images, the standard format for photographs. What you download from Flickr is usually a .jpg file. A .jpg image cannot have a transparent background.

- .gif images, a common format for drawings and logos; in this format, the number of different colors is narrower than in a .jpg file; image compression is based, among other things, on a kind of repertory that lists all colors used. Colors are said to be *indexed*. However, a .gif image can have a transparent background, and it can also be animated (it's the only widely used image format allowing animation). An animated image is in fact a small set of slightly different images displayed each one in turn, usually in a loop, in the same way that a film is a succession of still images.

- .png images, a format for all practical purposes close to the .jpg format, except that a .png image *can* have a transparent background. You can find many .png images on the web, and if you take a snapshot of your screen with Gimp it will create a temporary file in a .png format. It's the format in which I usually save edited images.

- .svg images, which are *vector* images and are a bit special. Like .gif images, they are used for drawings and logos and they support transparency, but they cannot be imported into PowerPoint (my version at least). Gimp can read a .svg image, but transforms it and cannot, once it's modified, write it back in the same format (to save an image in the .svg format you need a special program such as Inkscape). The other image formats basically store pixels; vector images are stored as instructions allowing to redraw the image – as a result, when with other formats enlarging the image too much causes the image to become ragged, .svg images can be enlarged without any loss of precision (svg stands for *Scalable Vector Graphics – Scalable* means that you can draw to any scale). Images on www.openclipart.org are vector images, and can be either downloaded as such, or as small, medium, or big .png image. When you open a .svg file in Gimp, it asks you for the size you want to give to the drawn image.

Additionally to these four image formats, I must mention .xcf files. This is the format used by Gimp itself. A .xcf file cannot be imported into PowerPoint, but if you are engaged in serious image revamping and cannot finish it in one go, you should save your image as a .xcf file that will keep all the layers you usually create when editing an image (more about layers later). Otherwise, you don't really need .xcf files. With the older versions of Gimp, you could use "Save as" and name the file with the extension corresponding to the format you want. Newer versions require using "Export" to save to another format than .xcf. In most cases, I export to .png files. It's unnecessary to save the image to a .xcf file once it has been exported, unless you want to keep on editing it.

When you have opened a file of any supported format, before you start anything you must check two settings, and make sure that you have three special windows on your screen (these requirements are summarized in Figure 4-6). The two settings are very important, because otherwise some options will appear disabled in the menus or may simply not work.

- The first important setting is to ensure, in the "Image" menu, that the mode is set to "RGB" (it means Red/Green/Blue and refers to how colors are encoded). It should normally be the case when you open a color .jpg or .png file. An image imported from a .gif file will be set to "Indexed" and this must be changed to RGB.

- The second setting is in the "Layer" menu, under "Transparency". If "Add Alpha Channel" is disabled and "Remove Alpha Channel" is enabled, everything is fine. Otherwise, click on "Add Alpha Channel." The Alpha Channel is just a fancy name to say that you can make some parts of the image transparent. The Alpha Channel is never enabled by default with .jpg files, with other formats it depends.

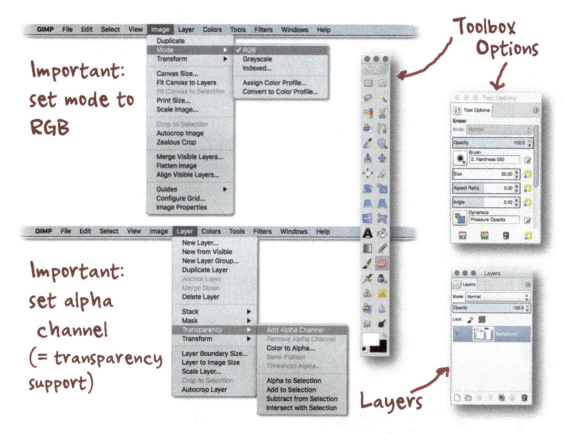

Figure 4-6. *A Gimp survival kit*

Before you start editing the image, you should have three special windows opened (they can be independent windows, they can sometimes be sub-windows). Some versions of Gimp open at least some of them automatically when you launch the program; other versions require opening these windows explicitly in the "Windows" menu.

The three windows are the following:

- The toolbox. Don't be impressed by the large number of icons; you'll mostly use five or six tools 99% of the time, and these tools are rather intuitive.

- The options box. Each tool as special options. I use the options window for basically one purpose: setting the size of the eraser and other similar tools when I work on an image, big for large areas, and small for tiny details.

- The layers box. You can have layers when editing images in the very same way that you have layers in PowerPoint as you have seen in the previous chapter. Layers are very useful for a number of operations (you'll see soon several examples). When you open a .png or a .jpg file, you always have a single layer. You can see in Figure 4-6, in the "Layer" menu, options for creating a new layer (which can be transparent, white, or in the default background or foreground color), or duplicating the current one. Layers can be used as drafts when you are unsure about your result. A layer can be merged into the layer below it. The layers box lets you define the currently active layer (by clicking on it), or make a layer visible or invisible (by clicking to its left). You can also move layers up and down the stack or delete them using buttons at the bottom of the box. When you save to a .png or .jpg file, the resulting image will contain a single layer, obtained by merging.

Once those checks are performed and these windows opened, you are ready to go. Don't hesitate to experiment. Gimp allows you to undo any change, and is very tolerant of missteps.

Filters

You have seen in the previous pages how to use PowerPoint filters to hide the low resolution of an image that you want to use from edge to edge. My favorite filter for this purpose isn't one of the PowerPoint filters but a Gimp filter, to be found in the "Filters" menu under "Artistic" and is called "Oilify." You can see its result in Figure 4-7.

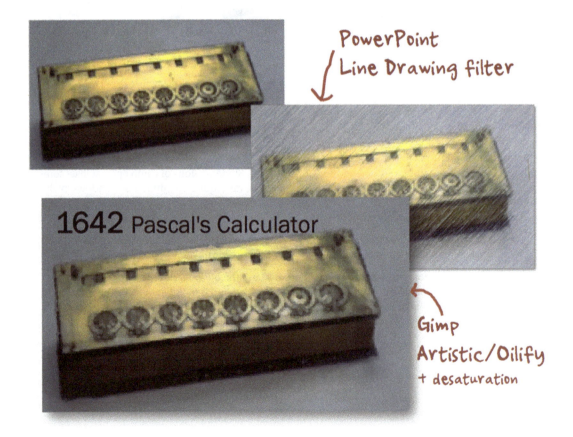

Figure 4-7. *Filters, Gimp vs. PowerPoint*

This filter transforms a photograph into a mock oil painting by turning pixels into small spots of color that blend into neighboring spots. The size of spots is adjustable, which allows getting more or less detail. I have also used, under the "Colors" menu, the "Hue-Saturation" option to desaturate colors a little, which means making them a tad grayer.

Image Correction

I have shown in Figure 4-2 how to remove in PowerPoint the background from Marcin Wichary's picture of the Pascaline. However, I have pointed out that the acrylic support, which is understandable within the full image, looks like a foreign element when taken out of context. What about removing this acrylic support from the image? This operation can be effected reasonably fast and easily with Gimp. I have illustrated the process in Figure 4-8, and I have only used three Gimp tools to do it. Image 1 in Figure 4-8 shows one support I want to remove (as you can see, I have zoomed on the picture). It's not too visible in the figure, but the support half-hides what looks like the head of a copper nail. You can see another head of copper nail on the right-hand side of the picture, and this is where I'm going to collect a "patch" to hide the piece of acrylic support. The first tool I'm using is actually the first one in the tool box, "rectangle select." I have drawn in image 2 a small rectangle around what will become my patch. The tiny rectangle in the corners of the dotted rectangle are hot spots, handles allowing me to size precisely my patch, so that it's neither too small nor too big. Once I'm satisfied, I can got to "Edit/Copy" and "Edit/Paste" in the menu (or use keyboard shortcuts) and you see the result in image 3: the patch is created as a new temporary layer above its original location.

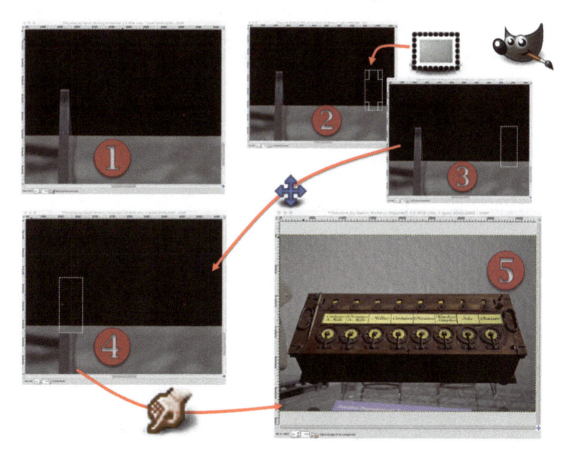

Figure 4-8. Removing acrylic supports from the Pascaline picture.

At this stage I must use the "move" tool (the pointed cross), click on the patch, and bring it into position as shown in image 4. There was a very small luminosity difference; the patch was just a little lighter than its new surroundings. I have adjusted luminosity using the "Brightness-Contrast" option under the "Colors" menu, then I have applied my patch using, under the "Layer" menu, "Anchor layer"; the effect of this option is to merge the currently pasted piece into the layer beneath it (the other choice you have with a pasted piece is to turn it into a permanent layer of its own, using an option that only appears in the "Layer" menu when you have pasted an image, "To New Layer"). The icing on the cake is obtained with the "Smudge" Gimp tool, represented by a hand with an extended finger, and it will allow you to smooth the limits and remove any straight line resulting from the paste operation; you may need to adjust the 'brush size' in the Tool Options window. Rinse, repeat for every support, and you can see the final result in image 5 (I have also removed, using the same technique, a glare on the left-hand side of the calculator that was appearing like a lighter spot on the wood).

The picture is now ready for the next step: removing the background.

Background Removal

Background removal, while not difficult, takes a little time, and you may encounter a few thorny issues. The case of the Pascaline, though, is relatively easy. The first stage is shown in Figure 4-9; in image 1, I use the rectangle select tool, once again, to frame the now support-less calculator reasonably closely. In the "Image" menu, "Crop to Selection" reduces the image to the selected area. After having zoomed on the photograph, I use in image 3 the "free select" tool, represented by a lasso icon in the toolbox. You can either keep the left button down and follow the edges, or, which I always do, click once and release the mouse button, move the mouse, thus drawing a line segment, then click once again whenever I change direction to enclose any area. When you are nearing your point of departure, click twice and the tool will complete the loop by itself.

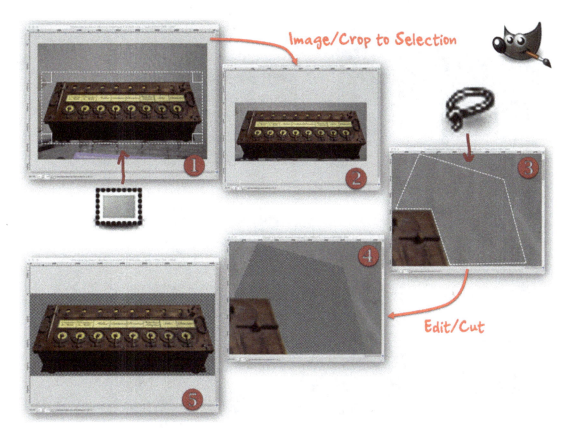

Figure 4-9. *Background removal with Gimp, stage 1*

Then, "Cut" in the "Edit" menu will remove the enclosed area and make it transparent, because you didn't forget to add the Alpha Channel. If you did, the enclosed area will become a plain area in the background color. It's not too late, though; you can still add the Alpha Channel and repeat the cut operation. A transparent area appears as a gray checkerboard in Gimp. Alternatively, you can try to draw, with the "free select" tool, the outline of the calculator, then go to the "Select" menu and choose "Invert," the result of which will be to select the area that is *not* enclosed, thus allowing you to cut it all at once. I find the method I have first exposed easier, if a little longer. In the end, you end up with something looking like image 5 in the figure.

You might consider that you are done if your purpose is to put the processed image on a background the color of which is very close to the original background color in the photograph. Generally, though, it won't be the case. Stage 2 of the process is shown in Figure 4-10.

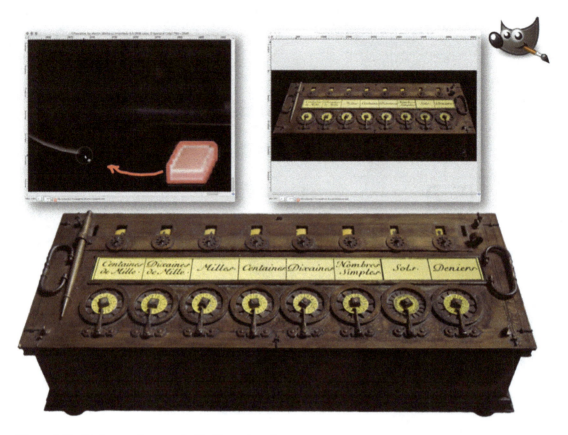

Figure 4-10. *Background removal with Gimp, stage 2*

Go to the "Layer" menu and choose "New Layer." The window that opens asks for a layer fill type, and you should select either the foreground or the background color (both are visible at the bottom of the toolbox). Assuming the default values (black foreground, white background), you should select the foreground color if the original background was light, and the background color if it was dark – simply put, choose the color that contrasts most with the original background. In my case I have added a black layer. It's created above the image I am editing, and I must use the arrows in the layers box to move it at the bottom, then I must click on the layer corresponding to the image to make it the active layer again.

What you'll see then will be like what you have in the top left in Figure 4-10: a kind of white halo all around the image. You should remove this halo with the eraser tool. By default, the eraser is a round "brush" with soft edges, which works very well for this kind of work; you may want to adjust the brush size in the Tool Option windows. This stage is the longest one. Once everything looks neat on the black background, delete the black layer, and export the image as a .png file. You see the result at the bottom of Figure 4-10.

Processing a simple geometric shape, moreover on a clean background, is usually relatively quick and easy. Background removal isn't always, though, a bed of roses. I prove it with Figure 4-11, a photograph of a doll in the likeness of the child actress that every little boy born in the early 1930s was secretly dreaming of marrying when he grew up: Shirley Temple. To the risk of shocking a number of respectable elderly gentlemen (and of little girls), this photograph is, from an image editing standpoint, absolute evil.

Figure 4-11. *The nightmare*

The background shows through the hair, and on the left-hand side it gave purple reflections that will look completely out of place when the background is removed. You can obtain a relatively decent image in a few operations, as illustrated in Figure 4-12 on one of the scariest parts of the photograph.

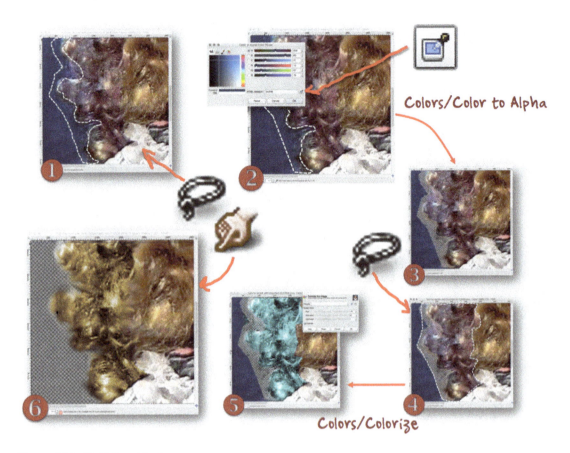

Figure 4-12. *To Hell and back*

Step 1 consists in using the "free select" tool (the lasso) to circle the part in the hair where the background shows through. Step 2 consists in going to the "Colors" menu and choosing "Color to Alpha"; you remember that "Alpha" is just a shorter name for "transparent." The window suggests, by default, to turn white to transparent. Double-click on the white rectangle after "From:"; and a new window opens allowing you to change the color that will become transparent. In this window, you have a color-picker to the right of a field named "HTML notation." Click on this tool to pick the background color. As background colors aren't usually uniform, you should aim for an average, mid-tone color that is representative of the background as a whole.

Once you have selected the color to make transparent, click OK. You see the result in step 3; it will be messy, because backgrounds aren't areas of solid uniform color (and there were hairs too).

In step 4, select again more or less the same area with the "free select" tool, but expand it so as to include all the hair area that is purple because of the background and light reflections. We are going to change the color in this area, using, under the "Colors" menu, the "Colorize" choice. You see what happens in step 5, it immediately turns the area to a light teal color, but don't panic; teal is the default Gimp color for this tool. First, adjust the "Hue" slider to come as close as possible to the color of hair outside the selected area. Then fine-tune with the "Saturation" and "Lightness" sliders. When the color is right and you have accepted it for the current selection, go to the "Select" menu, choose "All" to cancel the selection, and use the "Smudge" tool (finger) to adjust the former limits, and to fluff that part of hair that should let the background appear through. The final result is shown in step 6 (I have also cleaned up the background), and you can compare it to step 1. Phew.

There were in Figure 4-11 large areas where colors had a wrong tint. What happens most often, especially when the original background is a bright color and what you want to keep is either dark or light, is color bleed in the photograph: the edges of what you want to keep have "absorbed" the background color. It's hardly perceptible with the background, but it looks wrong when the original background is removed. A simpler way than "Colorize" to fix the color of narrow areas is to circle them with the "free select" tool, then simply remove every hint of color with, in the "Colors" menu, "Desaturate." The selected area will take the right shade of gray and will pass unnoticed, often even without even any need for "smudging."

Preparing Portraits

I like to show portraits of people I'm talking of. I'd never consider talking of the Pascaline without showing Blaise Pascal. You've seen a bust of him in Figure 4-2, but it's not the type of portrait that you can easily mix with the calculator picture.

Portraits of authors or scientists who lived prior to the mid-19th century are often available as engravings or lithographs (books used to contain the portrait of the author in the first pages). These old pictures are easy to process, and easy to use; however, as they are usually scanned from old books, they may be on the small side. I easily found on the web a lithography representing Blaise Pascal, but it's a small image. Its processing is shown in Figure 4-13 (the background of the figure isn't white so that you can distinguish white from transparent). I started at step 1 with an image in the .jpg format (no transparency), which is only 300 by 314 pixels. This image has a pure white background. Sometimes you find color pictures taken from old books, with for background a yellowish paper. In that case you can use, in the "Colors" menu, the "Desaturate" option that turns the image into shades of gray, then, still in "Colors," "Brightness-Contrast" to increase both brightness and contrast and obtain a white background.

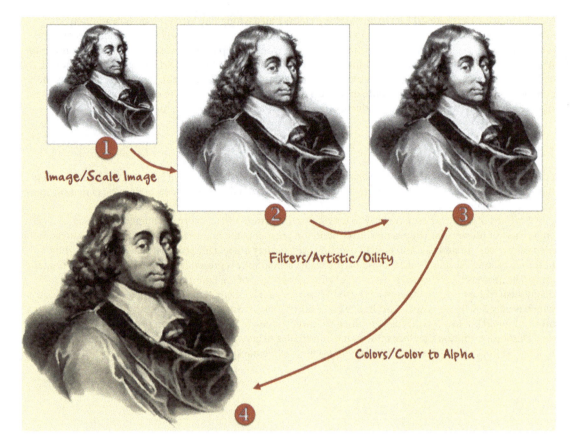

Figure 4-13. *Making an engraving or lithography suitable for inclusion in a slide*

As the picture is too small, I have enlarged it using, under the "Image" menu the "Scale Image" option, and I have turned it into a 600 by 628 image (step 2). Of course, making the picture four times bigger – Figure 4-13 isn't to scale - does nothing to improve resolution, and irregularities are beginning to show in the image. It's time for camouflage, and I'm using in step 3 the magic wand of the "oilify" filter, with a spot size just sufficient to hide irregularities. Finally, I turn white to transparent (it's the default option) using, in the "Colors" menu, the option "Color to Alpha."

At this stage, it doesn't matter if you have forgotten to add the Alpha channel: "Color to Alpha" automatically adds it.

The resulting image (step 4) must be exported to a .png file and can be used over any light background. As you can see, you obtain a correct image (which can be made reasonably big) in what is in practice a matter of seconds.

Now, for a number of reasons (dark background, consistency with the other slides), you may prefer a color portrait, which means, for a 17th-century person, a painting. A web search returns many pictures, but there are very few different pictures of Pascal (most of them posthumous, moreover – they may be partly based on his death mask). As a result, options are rather limited and I have settled for the portrait in Figure 4-14. The big weakness of this portrait is that, even if you increase as much as you can the size of the image, it's impossible to distinguish hair from background. The fact that no ears are visible eliminates the crew-cut option, but otherwise you really have to guess. Resisting the temptation of a quiff, I wisely modeled the hairstyle after the black and white lithography, and removed the background using the method presented in the previous pages.

Figure 4-14. *Hairdo guesswork*

At this point, there is one important point to notice: slide layout is far easier with the lithography than with the processed painting of Figure 4-14. The reason is that there is a straight line at the bottom of the processed painting, which forces alignment of the portrait with the bottom edge of the slide. Contrast it with the lithography, with its soft lower part: we can place it virtually anywhere within the slide (at least on the left-hand side, as the face is turned to the right; if we want to place the portrait on the right-hand side, we'll have to flip it).

In some cases, aligning a portrait along the edge isn't a big issue; for instance, in a quote slide, where the portrait of the author is the focus of attention, it can occupy a large area of the slide. In other cases, being able to "float" a portrait is definitely an asset. If a portrait has to be aligned on the bottom edge, you cannot give it any size you want on the slide; its height must be at least something around two-thirds of the height of the slide; otherwise the portrait will give the impression of having sunk to the bottom.

If I mention, in the course of a talk, a scientist associated with an important result, I definitely want to show a portrait of this scientist, but the focus is on the important result; I don't want the portrait to take up most of the surface. This is the reason why I transform most portraits so as to have a "soft lower part" reminiscent of engravings of centuries past that gives me far more freedom for sizing the portrait and placing it on the slide.

Creating a soft lower part makes an intense usage of layers, but it isn't particularly complicated and is shown in Figure 4-15 (I have used the same background as in Figure 4-13 for the same reason, helping you distinguish white from transparent).

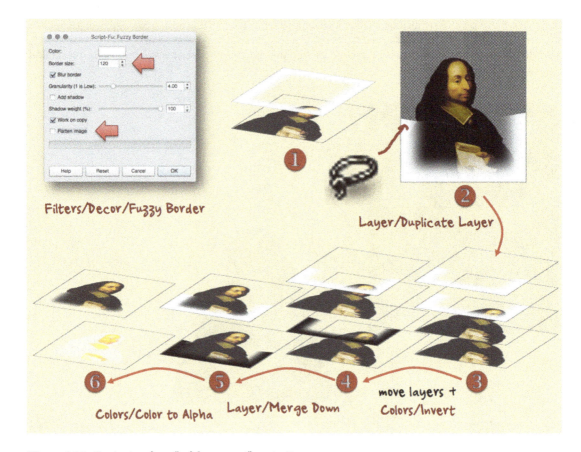

Figure 4-15. *Basic steps for a "soft lower part" portrait*

It starts with the portrait on a transparent background, and a special filter called "Fuzzy Border" found in a "Decor" submenu of the filters. When you select this filter, a window pops up and you must change two of the default options (thick red arrows in Figure 4-15). The first option is the border size. Set it, approximately, to about 1/7th or 1/8th of the smallest dimension of the visible image; in my experience this is what works best. The second option is a box that you must uncheck: "Flatten Image." By default, the process that creates a fuzzy border creates intermediate layers and merges them into one at the end; for creating a soft bottom layer we need to omit this last step. Running the filter will now create a new image with two layers as shown at step 1: the original image at the bottom, and a kind of fuzzy white frame on top. Step 2 consists in removing the part of this mask that is, roughly, above the shoulders. Use the "free select" tool (lasso), not anything linear (there is an "ellipse select" tool that could be used too). Edges will be softened only where the mask remains. Once you have done this, don't forget to go to "Select" and "All" because the next steps will be applied to entire layers.

At step 3 you must duplicate *both* layers, the fuzzy frame and the original image. Select one of the fuzzy frames, then turn it from white to black by selecting "Invert" under the "Colors" menu.

You must then use the arrows at the bottom of the Layers box to place the four different layers as shown at step 4: white fuzzy frame on top, a copy of the original image, black fuzzy frame and at the bottom the other copy of the original image. Make the white fuzzy frame the current layer, then in the "Layer" menu select "Merge Down." Repeat the operation with the black fuzzy frame, so as to obtain the two layers shown at step 5. Select the top layer, and use under "Colors" "Color to Alpha" to make white transparent; then select the bottom layer, and make black transparent. The result is shown at step 6.

I have not illustrated a few additional steps that are required:

- The resulting image is very transparent. I usually take the bottom ghost-white layer, duplicate it twice, and merge the three resulting white layers into a single one. It gives a bit more substance to the white layer. I am *not*, at this stage, merging the blackish layer with them.

- As I do with background removal, I create a black layer and put it at the bottom of the stack. You will usually notice a halo effect around the image. Make the white layer (middle layer) the current one, and remove the halo using the eraser. Once this is done, you can delete the bottom black layer and merge the two remaining layers.

- Colors will need to be adjusted. You have removed white from the picture, and you have removed black from the picture: when you put the two together, it means that you have removed gray. If desaturating an image is making colors grayer, removing gray has the opposite effects: it saturates colors. For a portrait, it's rather unfortunate because the soberest of men ends up looking like a boozer. You must, in the "Colors" menu, select "Hue-Saturation" and desaturate colors, adjusting manually so as to retrieve the original color (in the case of the Pascal portrait I have actually desaturated a bit more, as the original portrait looks a bit like a bad case of jaundice).

I use this method not exclusively for portraits. If you take a close look at Figure 4-6 in this chapter, which shows Gimp menus, you will see that the extremities of the menu bars are faded: I have applied exactly the same steps as explained above to screenshots, after removing the background.

I have used the modified portrait, in Figure 4-16, to show what a slide about the Pascaline could be. The figure doesn't claim to be a masterpiece of slide design, but a mere showcase for the images the edition of which was the topic of this chapter. As you can see in this figure, the portrait of Pascal is free to go almost anywhere on the left-hand side; I could also make it as small as I want or as big as resolution permits. Applying the lessons of John McWade, I haven't tried to include it entirely into the slide, but I have let it spill outside and I cropped the image. The desaturation of colors makes the portrait recoil in the background (a lesson from Bruce Block's *Visual Story*) and gives some depth to the slide. The star of the show is not Pascal but the Pascaline, free from any background and which I have tried to make as big as possible. There is no fancy effect such as a shadow, just the plain photograph. I'd like to point out that background removal is what allows blending on the same slide Pascal and Pascaline, two really heterogeneous pictures (painting and photograph). Adding Blaise Pascal over the edge-to-edge, unprocessed image of the calculator wouldn't work, unless perhaps you use the portrait as the background for an ellipse shape put over the picture, turning this portrait into a kind of vignette. I far prefer Figure 4-16 to the vignette solution. The slide is completed with very little text written in two fancy "period" fonts that put the viewer in the mood (I have used two different fonts because my choice for writing the text was AquilineTwo but I don't find digits very legible in that font).

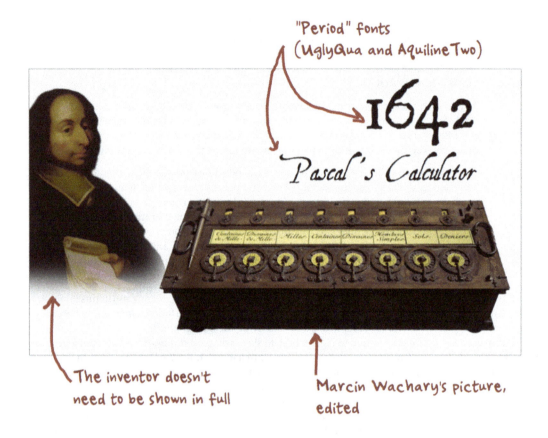

Figure 4-16. *What the final slide could be*

I end up with a slide that is very legible, in spite of fancy fonts, and that anybody can see well, even from the last ranks. A slide you can talk on, and a good support to explain that this calculator was invented by a 19-year-old to help his father, a tax collector, in his job, and that he had it built by a local clockmaker.

How Far to Go

As a conclusion to this chapter, and before moving on to the dynamics of a presentation, I'd like to give a few elements of answer to a practical question: image editing may require some effort, is it worth it? The first thing to say is that the amount of time may vary widely, depending on what you do, and depending also on the image. Adding a soft lower edge to an image, which may look complicated when you discover it for the first time, is an easy operation that with a bit of practice you can perform in a couple of minutes or less. Background removal in Gimp can be easy with regular shapes, and rather tough with fluffy, curved shapes (a case that the PowerPoint tool cannot handle). A second thing to say is that finding the right image usually takes far more time than editing it (of course, these times add up).

Must we spend twenty minutes working on an image that will be displayed for twenty seconds? My touchstone is how many people will see the edited image. If your presentation is a one-time event before four people, it's probably not worth your time, unless the outcome of your presentation will determine your professional activities for the next five years. If you expect your image to be seen over time by 1,000 people (not necessarily in a single presentation, good images deserve recycling), then twenty seconds time

1,000 amounts to five and one-half hours, and twenty minutes no longer seem shocking. I apply the same reasoning to some operations that you'll see in the next chapters, which may be time consuming too.

My point of view is that details count in a presentation, and you'll never get anything else than a mediocre result if you don't pay attention to them. It's better to show no image rather than a bad one.

Summary

In this chapter we covered the topics:

- There are several options for placing images on a slide, which also depend on the resolution of available images.

- A handful of PowerPoint tools are available for background removal and hiding low image resolution.

- Image editing tools such as Gimp let you better process images for a presentation: you can correct a few defects in an image; remove a background by hand; and make the bottom part of a portrait fuzzy so that you place it wherever you want in the slide, and at any size you want.

Now that we know how to improve each slide, let's see in detail how we link slides together.

CHAPTER 5

■ ■ ■

Transitions

Look on every exit as being an entrance somewhere else.

—Tom Stoppard (1937-)

The previous chapters have mostly been about designing, in the wider sense, a single slide. I pointed out in Chapter 2 that the idea, not the slide, should be the unit, and that you can organize one idea into a natural flow of slides. This chapter and the following ones are devoted to improving the flow, and this one will be more precisely dedicated to switching from one slide to the next. It may seem the simplest of topics; but as you'll see, it actually deserves some reflection.

Thinking Transitions

Most people just keep the default behavior in their slide decks: no transition, in other words when you "advance," the next slide simply replaces, all at once, the slide that precedes it. This naive approach is in my view far better than trying to use transitions to pep up a presentation that the author finds too dull. I have attended long ago an IT presentation by a speaker who was young and enthusiastic, had a sense of humor, and knew very well what he was talking about. He made only one mistake, but a capital one: he chose to have random transitions between his rather static slides. Even he seemed surprised every time he was advancing to the next slide. His presentation should have been one of the good talks at this conference, and all I could remember was this major mistake of random transitions. You could see nothing but them. In fact it remained a trauma for me, so much that I decided that transitions were better avoided, and I didn't use them for many years, using animations instead.

When your goal is to make your presentation lively, the key is to see movement as an integral part of the story, and not as a gimmick to try to instill life where there is none. You have the same issue with software such as Prezi, which wants to be an alternative to PowerPoint. Prezi gets rid of the photographic slide paradigm that powers other presentation software, and lets your audience view your presentation as a kind of large virtual panel on which you zoom and where you move the focus from place to place. The concept is interesting, but in practice I find Prezi more limiting than traditional presentation software, and unsuitable for presentations that are longer than 30 minutes. If it's possible to create a PowerPoint presentation that doesn't look like a PowerPoint presentation (I'm trying to prove it), I find it far more challenging to create a Prezi presentation that doesn't look like a Prezi presentation. I've seen Prezi presentations that were in every way as bad as PowerPoint presentations, but with added motion sickness. I'm not sure that it's an improvement.

The goal with any medium is finally to arrive at a state where the medium, having served its purpose of transmitting information, fades into oblivion, and the person on the receiving end remembers the information, and not the medium. Sometimes you don't remember about a piece of information whether you heard it on the radio, saw it on TV, read about it in a paper or on the Web, or whether it was told to you by someone. You just know it. Forgetting about the source is definitely worrying when it comes to assessing credibility, but in terms of transmission of information, I see such a situation as the ideal to move toward.

Transitions and Animations

My standpoint on transitions changed one day when I wanted to talk about networks, and explain that in a computer network, at least with the TCP/IP protocol that is used over the Internet, every message is a small packet. You need about two of them for a single text page, and when you want to send something big – for instance, multimedia content – it's sliced at one end and reassembled at the other end.

To represent the network, I used a cylinder shape, which I rotated and colored with a gradient to make it look more like a pipe. To represent something big, to hell with clichés, I used a fun elephant clipart.

My goal was to make the elephant disappear on the left-hand side of the pipe, and to have the same image on the right-hand side appearing at the same time as shown in Figure 5-1. Additionally, I wanted both appearance and disappearance to give the visual idea of the big element sliced into small packets.

Figure 5-1. *Network transmission*

Presentation software features many animations allowing elements to appear or disappear on a slide, and we'll see them in some detail in the next chapter. Unfortunately, I explored all of them and couldn't find any one rendering what I wanted. I didn't want the elephant to disappear and appear suddenly. I excluded fade out and fade in that would carry out an idea of vaporization. The "dissolve" effect looked like a "pixie dust" effect. What came closest to what I wanted was a "checkerboard" effect, which was unfortunately missing the randomness that I was looking for to express that packets, as they may take different routes, don't necessarily arrive in order.

I was stranded without an idea. I don't remember why I turned my attention to transitions (despair, probably). Many transitions bear the same name as an animation, and I have already pointed out in Chapter 2 that in many cases, using animation on one slide or transitions across a succession of different slides is a mere question of personal technique. However, there are sometimes slight visual differences between similarly named transitions and animations; I noticed that with the animation called "dissolve" pixels were vanishing, while with the transition called "dissolve" the transition was operating on little squares, which was exactly what I was looking for.

When you define a transition for a slide, it defines how you switch from the preceding slide to the current one, not how you move away from the current slide. In some versions of PowerPoint, transitions are depicted by small icons with a slide called A and a slide called B; the current slide is always B (I'll adopt this type of icon in this book). Generally speaking, the darker hue in icons represents the current slide, and the lighter hue represents the preceding slide.

I had the idea of replacing the slide in Figure 5-1 by two successive slides, the first one with the elephant on the left, the second one with the elephant on the right as illustrated in Figure 5-2, and I set the transition between the two slides to "dissolve." The result I obtained was exactly the effect I had been looking for.

What surprised me when I tried this sequence of slides, even if on second thought it makes perfect sense, is that the pipe is in no way affected by the transition. I wouldn't have been surprised by seeing the pipe unchanged without a transition between the two slides, or with a faded transition, but I wasn't expecting the same result with a transition that looks much fancier. With "dissolve," like with no transition or with "fade," the transition only shows what differs in both slides.

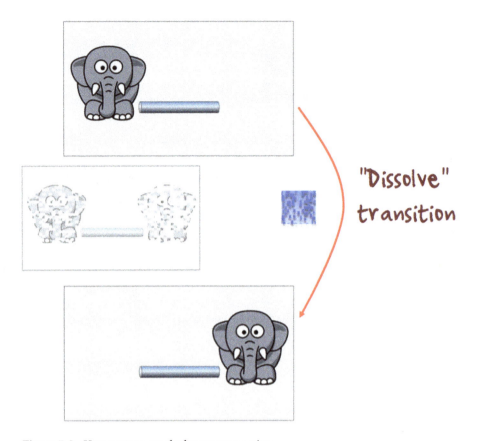

Figure 5-2. *How to move an elephant across a pipe*

Classifying Transitions

I suddenly understood that, although this behavior isn't universal, there were other transitions in addition to substitution and fading that could be perceived not as a switch from one slide to the next, but as a special type of animation. The characteristic of these transitions is that if two successive slides have common elements, when the transition is set on the second slide, nothing that is common will seem affected. In fact, if I had two successive identical slides, I would see nothing at all when switching from one to the other.

As long at this characteristic allows us to change slides as smoothly as we want, it seemed to me far more important to classify transitions in two main classes: transitions that present this characteristic and transitions that are always noticeable, rather than using "Subtle," or "Exciting" as suggested by PowerPoint ("Dynamic Content" is in a category of its own and I'll discuss it shortly).

I didn't know how to name transitions that are invisible between two successive slides, and I decided on an adjective borrowed from mathematics to call them *idempotent transitions*. In mathematics, an idempotent element changes nothing to the result of a given operation, such as 0 for addition or 1 for multiplication.

I have illustrated in Figure 5-3 the various transitions available in my version of PowerPoint (yours may differ slightly and contain more, and fancier, transitions) and I have appended a green check to every transition that is idempotent (and a red cross to every transition that isn't). As you can see, most transitions in the "subtle" category are idempotent, but not all of them, and if the majority of "exciting" transitions aren't idempotent; two of them are – "dissolve" in particular.

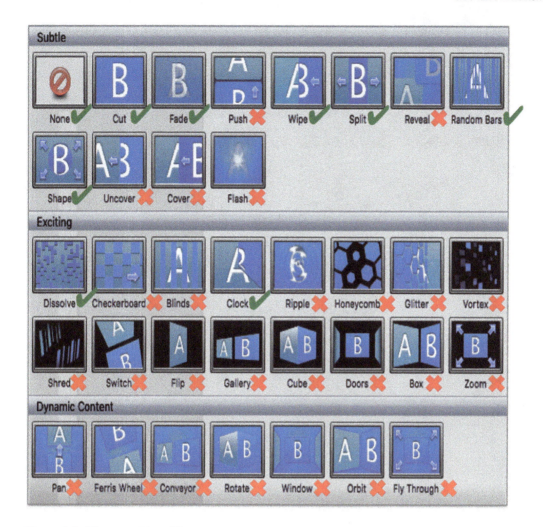

Figure 5-3. *Idempotent transitions*

None of the "Dynamic Content" transitions are idempotent, because they move objects on the slide. "Dynamic Content" works like regular transitions applied to slides on a transparent background, on top of an immovable visible background. "Dynamic Content" transitions mirror other transitions where background and objects move together: "Pan" corresponds to "Push," "Ferris Wheel" corresponds to "Switch," and so forth (fortunately icons have a family look). The only other difference is that "Dynamic Content" moves end up with a slight rebound effect.

If you remember Chapter 2, and sequences of slides that are undistinguishable from a single, animated slide, any idempotent transition is a potential candidate when your purpose is to give continuity to the visual illustration of your talk. In Chapter 2, I illustrated how you could bring in the intercept theorem in a full sequence of slides. Figure 5-4 details a point I mentioned in passing in Chapter 2: if it makes sense to use animation to make the schema appear piece by piece (it could also be done with successive slides),

I suggested using a "wipe from left" transition between the two slides. Because this transition is idempotent, the only perceptible change will be the appearance of the line of ratio equalities, which will be displayed as indicated by the light blue arrow of Figure 5-4.

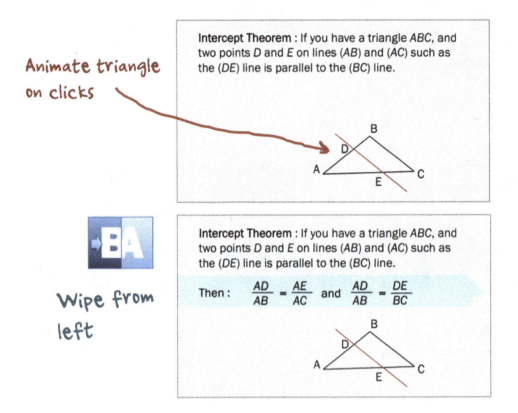

Figure 5-4. Revisiting the intercept theorem presentation

The point to be careful about is whether the transition has a "starting point" and an "ending point" or affects the whole slide at once. For instance, "Cut" (in practice, same as no transition), "Fade," "Random Bars," and "Dissolve" all affect the whole slide at once, while "Wipe," "Split," or "Cover" all have a "starting point" and an "ending point" (the direction can usually be altered). In the example of Figure 5-4, the wipe move starts from the left edge and goes all the way to the right edge; this is a major difference with the otherwise equivalent animation that we'll see in the next chapter, which starts on one side of the object and finishes when the opposite side is reached. A transition going from edge to edge may introduce a delay before the effect becomes visible, or before you proceed to the next effect. It's a point of no importance to the audience, who sees almost the same thing unless multiple animations are triggered in quick succession; it may be uncomfortable for the presenter. As a presenter, I like, whenever I press a button or a key to move to the next slide or to trigger an animation, to see my action immediately followed by a reaction. If not, I may think that I didn't press strongly enough and do it again, thus skipping accidentally an effect that may be important for supporting my explanation. When you factor in nervousness, it's easy to make a mistake.

In Figure 5-4, what will be displayed by the transition starts at 'Then.' The default time for the transition is 0.7 seconds (it's adjustable). The white space between the left edge of the slide and the 'T' is approximately 1/14th of the slide (I have measured it), which means that you'll see something after 5 hundredths of a second; it will "respond" instantly. However, if the object that must appear is located on the left-hand side, a delay of half-a-second may fool you into thinking that you didn't press the key strongly enough. It's not easy to remember the peculiarities of every transition in the 500 slides of a one-day seminar. The location of objects in the slide should therefore be a factor of choice both for the type of idempotent transition *and* for the direction, if a direction is relevant. If you want to reveal from left to right an object on the right-hand side, don't use "wipe from left," which starts from the left edge; use "split," which is idempotent too and starts from the middle of the slide. Aim to minimize the lag between your pressing a key and the appearance of the object.

As always, select a transition, even an idempotent one, which nobody will consciously notice because either it logically matches what it reveals or it corresponds to your topic. In Figure 5-4, wiping from the left works because what is revealed is text and it matches the sense of writing (unless you write in Arabic or Hebrew). "Random Bars" would be a gimmick. There may be cases when "Random Bars" is just the transition to use, but this case isn't one of them.

Accentuating a Break

I briefly mentioned "important breaks" in a presentation in Chapter 2, by which I meant true shifts in the talk, not simply signals to pay attention. Although an idempotent transition will not introduce a break by itself, you can perfectly use an idempotent transition to signal, say, a coffee break during a seminar. I have illustrated it in Figure 5-5, where a theater curtain falls to announce a break, and rises after the break, simply "animated" with two inverted transitions, wipe from top and wipe from bottom.

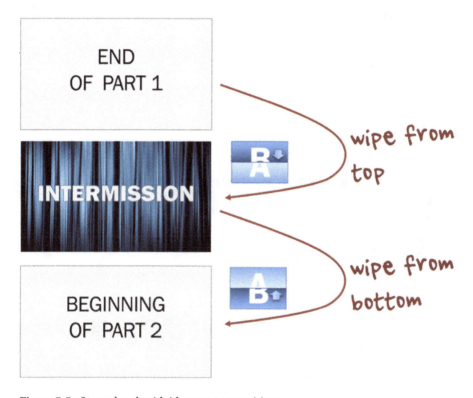

Figure 5-5. *Strong break with idempotent transitions*

When two successive slides contrast starkly, as is the case in Figure 5-5, the "wipe" transition doesn't give in my version of PowerPoint a very realistic feeling of a curtain falling or rising; there is a combined fading effect, which doesn't occur in LibreOffice Impress, for instance. If the effect isn't "realistic" enough for your taste, don't worry; you can make it more realistic with the animations of the next chapter.

It's a very simple effect, done in a matter of seconds, and it communicates instantly that everybody can unfasten the safety belt and walk away.

Non-idempotent transitions are very noticeable, and can only be used for breaks. Even so, avoid as usual anything too fancy. I would only use the "Ripple" effect if talking about hydrology or sound waves. I have already shown in Chapter 2 how two symmetrical, non-idempotent, transitions can be used for an aside: one non-idempotent transition to introduce the aside, the first one in a small collection of slides with possibly a different background, then the same non-idempotent transition as the one that brought the aside in, but in the opposite direction, to return to the main stream of the talk.

Figure 5-6 gives an example of a break between two different parts of a talk, when this break isn't associated with a pause. It also uses a symmetrical pair of non-idempotent transitions, reinforced with a technique that you'll see again in Chapter 7, a *fugitive slide*. In Figure 5-6, I'm using the transition called "shape." This transition belongs to a worrying category of transitions that are noticeable, but not blatantly noticeable. It's a transition close to a threshold that I could call "annoying distraction." Everybody will notice the change of slides, but not everybody may interpret it as your intent of marking a break; some people (perhaps because that's how they would use it themselves) may interpret the transition as a mere fun effect, especially if there are otherwise some elements of continuity (background, colors) between the two successive slides.

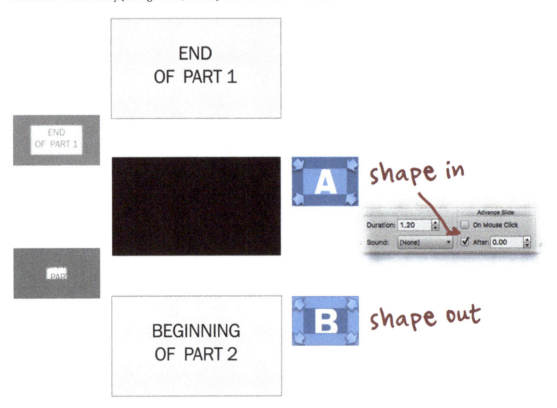

Figure 5-6. *Break with a non-idempotent transition and a fugitive dark slide*

I have inserted an additional dark slide (the darkest color in my Apress palette) that stresses that the transition is not a passing fancy of mine, but my way to establish a clear limit between two different parts of my talk. Visually, it will be a shrinking screen until everything is black immediately followed by a rectangle growing from the center; this type of transition is actually reminiscent of some transitions used in the films of the 1930s, as well as in George Roy Hill's 1973 classic, *The Sting*.

I mentioned earlier my using a fugitive slide; the dark slide is fugitive, because I don't want the screen to remain totally dark for more than a fraction of a second. As there is in that case no pause in my talk between parts 1 and 2, I don't want to press "next slide" once to switch from the slide inscribed "end of part 1" to the dark slide, then a second time to switch from the dark slide to the slide inscribed "beginning of part 2." I just want one a single-click move from part 1 to part 2, whatever is shown in between. This is why in the "Transition" panel for the dark slide, I have not only defined that I wanted to switch from the preceding slide to the present one using the "shape in" transition, but I have also specified that I want to advance automatically to the next slide after 0.0s: in other words, after the 1.2s that it takes for the transition to complete, plus, if there was any animation on the slide, the time it would take for all animations to complete.

Although it's possible to keep simultaneously automatic and mouse-triggered advance to the next slide, I always uncheck "On Mouse Click" whenever I create a fugitive slide; I don't want to interfere accidentally with a carefully prepared presentation. As a result of this setting, as soon as the "shape in" transition has run its course, we move to the next slide and "shape out" kicks in.

Other than asides and breaks between different parts, I also find non-idempotent transitions very useful when presenting alternate solutions, a frequent occurrence of technical talks. You start a first sequence of slides to present a solution to a problem, then use a transition such as "Gallery," "Switch," or "Flip" to start a new sequence corresponding to another solution, and finally use another non-idempotent transition to introduce a discussion of the pros and cons of the different solutions previously contemplated.

Whenever you are using a transition that isn't idempotent, what is important is that it fits your talk, and doesn't come out of the blue. I've illustrated in Figure 5-7 what I see as a fairly natural use of a transition that might look fancy – the "cube" transition (successive slides appear as faces of a rotating cube).

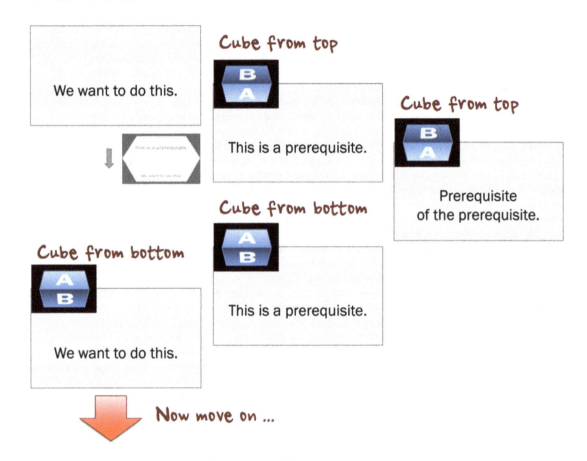

Figure 5-7. *When a fancy transition becomes part of the story*

The transitions are used to illustrate a case when what you present is subjected to one or several prerequisites, which may themselves be subjected to other prerequisites. In practice, it could be anything from the presentation of a curriculum to the milestones of a project. First you start by presenting what is probably the main focus of your audience. However, you can only do it if a prerequisite is satisfied. The "cube from top" transition will make the slide inscribed with "This is a prerequisite" come in from the top (remember that in my transition logos, B is the slide for which you are defining the transition), thus reinforcing the idea that it must come first. You can develop the idea, but then the prerequisite may itself have a prerequisite – "cube from top" again. Now, once you know what you need, you may "come back," with two successive "cube from bottom" transitions that will this time present the different steps or events in what is supposed to be the chronological order of execution, before coming back to the point of departure and moving on. It's important to review the sequence of operations as they are supposed to be performed. By only using pairs of symmetrical transitions, your audience can follow your presentation in the same way that it could understand a complex numerical expression with balanced parentheses. I don't feel any gimmickry in that case in the "cube" transitions – they are very much part of the story and correspond to a mental "stacking" and "unstacking," if I can allude to common operations in computer science.

Pushing the Boundaries

Among transitions that aren't idempotent, one deserves a detailed presentation of its own: the "push" transition. It's frequent in technical presentations to have at one point a lot of content to show: for instance, a hearty piece of computer code that needs to be dissected and commented. I have already told you in Chapter 3 how what I called "topic text" could and should be displayed as mouth-sized bits that the audience could chew on. Independently from presenting piece by piece, there may come a time where the "topic text" as a whole is too much to be presented with a legible size on a single slide. Take the problem any way you want, but you need to split your "topic text" over two or more slides. The question that interests us in this chapter is "how are we going to switch between slides that contain parts of a whole?"

I have seen most often presenters who follow the PowerPoint instructions ("Click to add title," "Click to add text") presenters write in the title box the name of the program they are explaining, and in the text box the first part of the program. On the next slide, they write again in the title box the name of their program followed by *(Continued)* or, more often, *(Cont'd)* - the big font size of titles incites to conciseness. Nothing really shocking here, but we are seeing slides setting the rhythm of the presentation instead of following it: because by definition both titles and slide contents will be different, idempotent transitions will be unable to provide any subtle continuity.

There are different ways to maintain continuity in such a case, and the simplest one is probably the "push" transition. I have illustrated it in Figure 5-8, where my code is actually a database query. Needless to say, both the first part of the query and the second part of the query should be displayed bit by bit. I'm just interested here in how to switch from part 1 to part 2. In practice, I would probably apply the transition to a slide containing only the first line of part 2, but I didn't want you to mistake it for an orphan line and wonder why I didn't try to squeeze everything on a single slide.

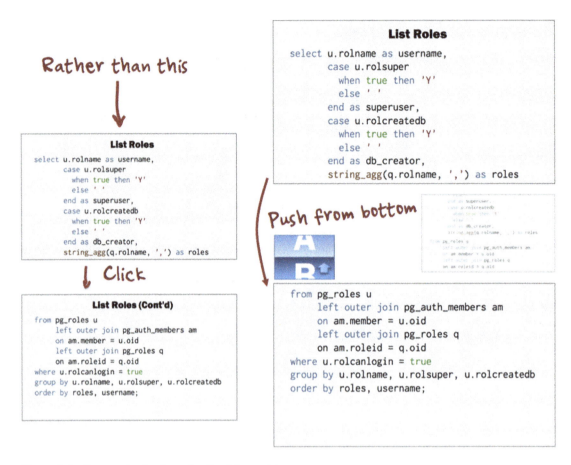

Figure 5-8. *Text continuity through a "push" transition*

The "push from bottom" transition will give the feeling of spanning along a single page that extends below the first slide. I mentioned at the beginning of this chapter the interesting concept in Prezi of a large virtual panel; "push" allows you in practice to give with PowerPoint a similar feeling of carrying a window along something that extends far beyond the boundaries of the visible slide.

There are two practical points to note with a "push" transition.

- The first one, which is more particularly linked to vertical transitions, is that you must take care of not having too wide a gap displayed on the screen between the text of both slides during the transition. Both the bottom margin on the first slide and the top margin on the second slide should be extremely narrow, because when the text scrolls you see, at the boundary of the two slides, a blank gap the width of which is the sum of the bottom margin of the first slide and of the top margin of the second slide. It works better when the audience would expect one or several blank lines at the point of demarcation (which isn't quite the case with the query in Figure 5-8, even if I have cut the query at what I'd consider a natural boundary, which explains unusually narrow bottom and top margins).

- I have already mentioned the second point in Chapter 1, when I warned that a fancy background, even something not wilder than a gradient, could become a burden in some cases. The "push" transition is what I had in mind. If you are using a linear gradient, you can only push *perpendicularly* to the gradient; otherwise two different colors will end up next to another and you'll see an ugly line flying across the screen; if the gradient isn't linear, you're entering Inferno and can abandon all hope. When your background contains a gradient that is unsuitable for a push (or when your background contains any kind of fancy graphics I disapprove of) you need to use the equivalent "Dynamic Content" transition, which is called "pan." The trouble with gradients and how to remedy it with the "pan" transition are both illustrated in Figure 5-9.

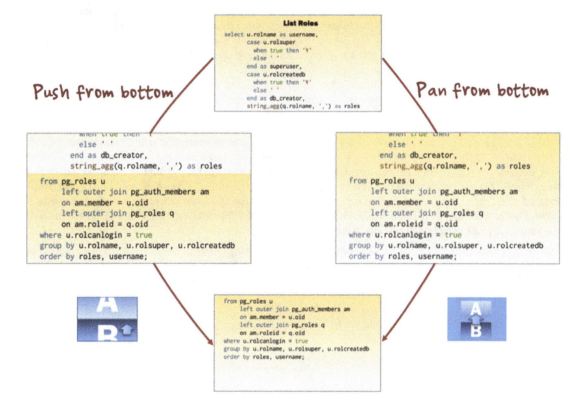

Figure 5-9. *The gradient background problem*

As you can see in Figure 5-9, if you push in the same direction as the gradient (left-hand side) the darker top color and the lighter bottom color, normally separated by a visually pleasing gradient, find themselves in brutal contact at the boundary between the two slides, which is disturbing; the only way to avoid it would be to reverse the gradient direction in the second slide, which might become a consistency issue with the remainder of the presentation. With "pan" (right-hand side), the equivalent "Dynamic Content" that moves slide contents over an immovable background, the problem vanishes because the background remains anchored. There is in my version of PowerPoint at the end of the "pan" a very slight rebound effect that is completely gratuitous and that I cannot suppress, but it's a lesser annoyance than the contrasted color boundary moving up across the slide.

The fixed background of "Dynamic Content," though, is in my view far more restrictive than a moving plain, uniform background. A gradient background, textured background, or any other background that isn't a solid color provides a visual point of reference: you see, from a fixed standpoint, text moving over a fixed background, and you unambiguously interpret it as text that scrolls up, not as the scope of your vision tilting down. When the background is uniform, you lose any spatial reference, and what happens is the same as when in a station one of two stopped trains starts moving very slowly: when you are in one of them, you cannot tell for a brief moment whether yours or the other train is moving. The uniform background gives you more latitude in the feeling you want to induce.

Contrary to what the name suggests, "pan" isn't at all like panning a camera over something that, as a landscape, doesn't move; it's with "push" associated with a plain background that you get that feeling. When the content is "dynamic," the point of view is less dynamic. And did I mention an annoying gratuitous rebound effect?

I suspect that "Dynamic Content" was introduced under pressure from the lobby of fancy background suppliers. However, you can often divert a feature from its original purpose and use it for something else; I'm going to give you an example that uses the plain background that I advocate, and combines it with the "pan" transition. More precisely, I'm going to give you an example that *seems* to use a plain background ... but doesn't.

In the previous examples of the "push" transition, the title ("List Roles" in the example) is an object that belongs to the first slide, and disappears with it. There is no repeated title on the second slide, because it would ruin the illusion of panning over a single piece of code. Yet, it might be a legitimate concern to want to keep, at least as a reminder, this title (a description of the purpose of the query) on every slide that shows code that is part of the query; however, as the title doesn't belong to the code, it shouldn't move with the code. Figure 5-10 shows a way to solve this problem. First, I found a place on the screen where my title could stay, even for the second slide in which the text must start pretty close to the top edge (remember that I don't want to see a big gap between the text of both slides during the transition). I chose the top right corner, and I created an empty slide with nothing but my title. Then I turned the slide into an image; you can either take a screenshot of it (I usually take screenshots with Gimp), or use the "File/Save as" menu of PowerPoint to save the slide as a .png or .jpg image, but check the options to make sure:

- That you only save the current slide,

- That the image size is big enough to have a good resolution (the smallest dimension must be at least in the 700 pixels range, preferably higher).

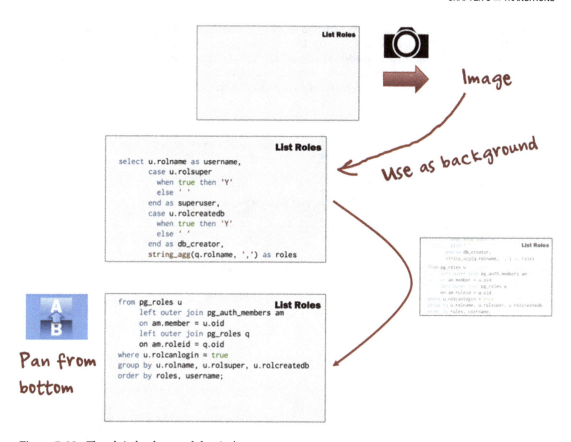

Figure 5-10. *The plain background that isn't*

Once you have this screen image with the title, you can use it as a new background for all the slides that contain pieces of related code: right-click on the slide background, select "Format Background," then click on the "Picture or Texture" tab in the window that opens to select the image. Now the title *looks* like the usual text object; but in reality it belongs to the background, and as such it won't be affected by the "Dynamic Content" pan. Code will flow, and the title will remain. I find that a single title over a plain background looks far less static than a fancy background: the title floats, but you still have a feeling of panning over text.

If the "push" transition (or the "pan" transition) allows scrolling, you aren't limited to a single direction. One of the most fascinating parts of Nancy Duarte's book *Slide:ology* explains how to narrate a story by moving along through push transitions. I have never really had the opportunity of using this technique for pure storytelling, but I'm going to show you how to apply something similar to a schema.

You probably remember the schema about nuclear waste that I have redone with shapes in Chapter 3. I have pointed out that, if my PowerPoint schema was readable, as opposed to the original one, it was far busier, because I had had to increase the size of every piece of text. Displaying the schema piece by piece in a presentation was like sugarcoating a bitter pill; but nevertheless my schema was far less elegant than the original one, only because, simply put, I had too much information on the surface of one slide.

I'm going to make the schema bigger than one slide, and present it by panning over it. How much bigger? For multiple reasons, some of which will be explained in a later chapter, four times is very convenient – perhaps would it be more correct to say "two by two" times bigger. The schema is a surface, we want to multiply each dimension by the same factor, and two is an easy factor to deal with. Conversely, each slide will represent a neat 25% of the whole, far more convenient than the 11.11111…% that it would represent if I were to multiply each dimension by three.

Figure 5-11 illustrates how I have proceeded to make my schema expand beyond the boundaries of a single slide. Starting with my busy slide at the top, I have separated it into four different quadrants. Then, I have rearranged the content of each quadrant to have one "area of interest" per slide. You see the result at the bottom, where each quadrant has become a slide to which I have assigned a letter. Quadrant C contains everything that regards fuel production; quadrant A is almost empty, and only refers to depleted uranium resulting from fuel production.

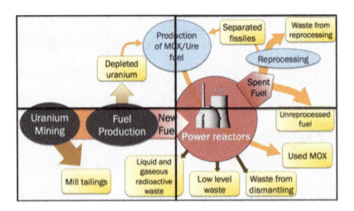

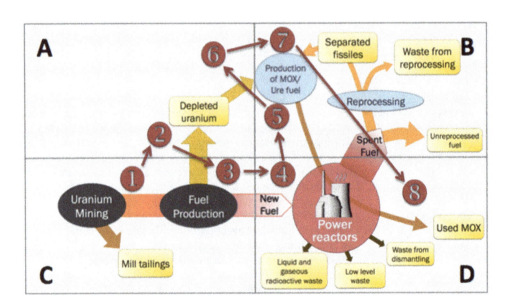

Figure 5-11. *Making the schema bigger than one slide*

Quadrants B and D are the busiest ones; quadrant D is about waste directly produced by the operation of a nuclear plant, while quadrant B is all about the reprocessing of spent fuel, some of which is recycled into the plant. I must once again stress that I haven't tried to balance the objects on my initial slide between the quadrants, I have just stretched the slide; there would be nothing wrong with an empty quadrant.

As you can see, when I split the schema over four slides, the resulting schema is far easier on the eyes, with the same (or bigger) font size. I'm far closer to the original schema shown in Chapter 3.

The bottom of Figure 5-11 also contains numbers and arrows showing how I'm going to walk the schema (as my only source of knowledge for this particular topic is this schema, I hope that readers who are more knowledgeable than I am will forgive any misinterpretation – my purpose is simply to illustrate a technique).

I'll start from quadrant C, showing fuel production, before a foray in quadrant A just to show the output of depleted uranium; at this stage, the slide won't contain the arrow pointing toward quadrant B. Back to quadrant C, before moving into quadrant D. Once quadrant D has been commented (without the "Used MOX" box and the arrow pointing to it), I'll move into quadrant B, then into quadrant A again to link it to the "Production of MOX" blue circle, then I'll show the arrow pointing back into quadrant D for the finale.

The main practical difficulty is to ensure visual continuity when an arrow extends from one quadrant into another, crossing the boundary. There are four such examples in Figure 5-11: the gradient arrow marked "New Fuel" expanding from quadrant C into quadrant D, the up yellow arrow expanding from quadrant C into quadrant A, the "Spent Fuel" short arrow expanding from quadrant D into quadrant B, and the curved orange arrow going down from quadrant B into quadrant D. The trick is that, although what you see is cropped so as to match the surface of a slide, nothing prevents you from having elements that extend past the slide area. Create an arrow, paste it on both slides it belongs to, and move it across the edges. I find that the easiest way for placing objects is right-clicking on the arrow, then choosing, depending on your version of PowerPoint, either "Size and Position" or "Format Shape" and then "Position": you can adjust either the horizontal or the vertical numerical position, which is more convenient for precise positioning than trying to drag the arrow with a mouse. A little trial and error and you can align very precisely elements that are common to two slides. Plain block arrows (such as the one extending up from quadrant C into quadrant A) are even easier – you just need a short arrow in quadrant A and a rectangle with a matching width in quadrant C.

To present the full schema, I chain the quadrant slides in the order of visit (as elements are added one after the other, the same quadrant will appear different as we progress). Switching from one quadrant to another is easy: if you are moving up, set the transition on the target slide to "push from top," and so forth. You always push from the direction where you want to go; that's what gives this feeling of moving. I have tried in Figure 5-12 to show the sequence of slides that you'll have in your slide deck, with the same quadrant letters and numbers as in Figure 5-11. The figure is a partial representation of the full set – I have let aside the display piece by piece of the different elements in a slide, skipping every step between the entrance into a quadrant and the exit from it to enter another quadrant. I'd like to point out, though, that sometimes a fugitive slide may precede a "push": whenever some kind of arrow starts from one quadrant to reach another quadrant, for instance, just before what I have marked as step 2, there is no reason to wait for a click and the move should be continuous, with an automated transition. I'd also like to point out, for the same step, that if a move such as the arrow going from "Fuel Production" in quadrant C into quadrant A would probably better performed with an animation – the topic of the next chapter – it's also possible to do it with a transition. I told you that you have to minimize the lag between your click and what you see on the screen. As the arrow starts from the top of the slide to move up (in this slide it's just a rectangle, the arrow head belongs to the next slide), a "wipe up" transition would probably look slow to the presenter. I have mentioned it earlier in this chapter: you can replace it with another idempotent transition, "split," which starts from the middle of the slide and moves toward the edges (or the reverse); such a transition reduces the delay before you see something moving on the screen.

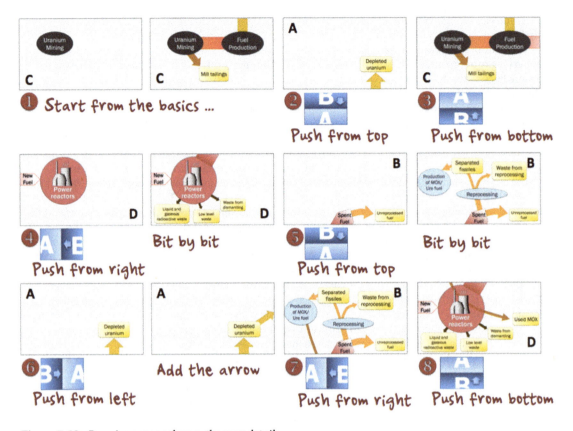

Figure 5-12. *Panning over a schema, the gory details*

At that point you may have a concern: everybody in the audience may not have a good spatial sense and some people, while following the progression, may have trouble mentally visualizing the schema in its entirety. What if we want, after panning on the details of the schema, to show a global view, for which legibility is no longer an issue? A question to which I can only make one answer: you haven't yet reached the end of this book.

Summary

In this chapter we covered the following topics:

- Transitions aren't a fancy way to make your presentation cooler, but are used for sequence continuity and for breaks.

- There are two categories of transitions: idempotent transitions that only affect elements that aren't common to two successive slides, and non-idempotent transitions that are always noticeable. The second category is used for breaks between parts of a talk or for asides; they can sometimes be used as a "part of the story."

- The "push" transition can be used for transforming the slide into a window over a much bigger pane.

- Dynamic content transitions, none of which are idempotent, affect object on the slides but not the background.

Transitions aren't the only way, though, to fit the rhythm of what occurs on screen to the rhythm of your speech: there are also animations, our next topic.

CHAPTER 6

Animations

Animation can explain whatever the mind of man can conceive.

—Walt Disney (1901-1966)

I have mentioned in the previous chapter that there were both similarities and differences between transitions and animations. I'll focus, while presenting animations in this chapter, on the differences: what you can do with animation that you cannot do with transitions. Although you can breathe life into a presentation only using transitions, there are two limits with transitions:

- Transitions reveal objects on a slide; they don't displace them. Dynamic content transitions only move the contents of the previous slide out of the screen to replace it with the contents of the current slide. You cannot move with a transition something, such as the image of a cursor, from position A to position B.

- As transitions operate on the whole slide, you cannot have two objects moving simultaneously but differently. Transitions are, by nature, sequential operations.

Animations allow (among other things) displacements across a slide and give you a far greater control of timing: you can fire several different animations at the same time or in very quick succession. Additionally, animation may respond a tad faster to your click as, for instance, "wipe" applied to an object starts from a side of the object, not from the edge of the slide. Although people who prepare business presentations are often suspicious of animations, they are extremely useful in technical presentations.

Why Animate

Making the contents of your slides move on screen, whether you are applying transitions or animations, should never be gratuitous. I see three reasons for dynamic slide content:

- Showing text or graphics as you are talking, to prevent your audience from being ahead of you and keep it interested (as far as your topic allows…).

- Showing a movement that belongs to the story – think of an animated schema, among other cases. It may be a simple or complex move, and I've given a few examples with transitions in the preceding chapter – using cube transitions for presenting prerequisites, and pushes to pan over a schema.

- Staging sequences, and playing on rhythm to improve continuity and flow; fugitive slides, which I've briefly introduced in the previous chapter, are just one example of how to make a presentation smoother.

© Stéphane Faroult 2016
S. Faroult, *Getting the Message Across*, DOI 10.1007/978-1-4842-2295-9_6

Matching visuals to the speed of your talk can be achieved simply with transitions; I have already talked about it in previous chapters. You can also – and it's really up to you – get a similar result with animations. You add animation to an object by selecting the object, then choosing an animation from the relevant menu. If you select a single element and animate it with "fade," a click will result in the same effect as a faded transition between a slide without the element and a slide that contains it. What and when to animate is dictated by your script, in the same way that in a play, scenes tell who's coming on stage and who returns backstage.

Moves that are part of the story come not from the rhythm in your script, but from your vision of what you want to explain. To use the play analogy again, it's about what happens on stage and how characters move in relation to each other. The key criterion might be the answer to the question: "If I had no PowerPoint and would explain this to somebody over a sheet of paper or in front of a white board, would I start scribbling arrows?" When you are craving for scribbling arrows, it means that when you talk, your visuals should move to express your thoughts; in most cases, you'll use animations rather than transitions. Another way of deciding when and how to animate is writing down what you plan to say, and then paying attention to the verbs you are using. When you are using linking verbs, such as "to be" or "to become" or verbs that suggest no move, it means transition. Dynamic verbs mean animation. Story-linked animation is far more necessary for a video, where people don't expect to be staring at a static image for too long, than for a presentation before a physical audience. During a live presentation you can gesticulate and balance static slides with body language. However, don't forget a criterion such as the size of the room, because from the back row the body language of an ant-sized presenter at the front of the auditorium doesn't help much. Don't forget, either, stage fright, optionally combined with jet lag, which can make you lose much of your gesticulatory capacities. When animations are built into your slide deck, you are safe.

The last point I have mentioned, staging sequences, is frankly more delicate and often requires the skills of a clockmaker. I have told it earlier: a sequence is a series of slides about the same idea, with elements that are common to several slides to provide continuity. Keeping an element from slide to slide doesn't necessarily mean that the element will stay in the same position from the first to the last slide in the sequence. You may want to put at one time the focus on one element, then perhaps leave it on the slide, because you know that you'll make casual references to it, but in a far less prominent position. To use once again the play analogy, the element is like downgraded from actor to part of the set; the set may also change between scenes.

Showing to your audience what you have in mind usually requires combining several techniques, and I'll demonstrate it in some detail in the next chapter. I often have a few animations on a slide; when I have too many, I use several slides and idempotent transitions to spread animations across slides. Combining animations and transitions helps with staging a complex visualization, and it makes maintenance easier – slide decks sometimes have to be updated or simply improved here and there.

The Grammar of Animations

The "Animations" tab in PowerPoint shows three possible categories:

- Appearance/Disappearance effects (called "Entrance/Exit effects" in PowerPoint, but the words "entrance" and "exit" suggest a movement that isn't always present). They go by pairs, each entrance effect being associated with a similar exit effect.

- Emphasis effects, a mixed bag of effects that alter the look of an object, either temporarily or up to the switch to the next slide.

- Motion paths, which take an object from one location on the slide and bring it to a different location on the same slide.

Difference between two different animations is sometimes subtle. If you create two rectangles, and associate an entrance "wipe" animation to the first one and an entrance "peek in" animation to the second one, you'll see when playing the slideshow two rectangles "growing" from their bottom edge (if you are using the default option). The only difference, and it's a subtle one, is that with "wipe" during the move the top edge will be blurry, whereas with "peek in" the blurry border will be the bottom one (which moreover will be slightly below the final position during the move) – this is at least what you'll see with PowerPoint; both effects will be undistinguishable in LibreOffice Impress. The real difference will only appear clearly when you add text inside the rectangle, or, even better, if you replace the rectangle with an arrow. I've done it in Figure 6-1, comparing an arrow wiped from left to right between two circles marked "A" and "B," and an arrow "peeking in" from left in a similar configuration. "B" should really be displayed after the arrow animation. I have shown in gray how everything was placed on the slide and how it will appear when animations have completed. The difference becomes clear with arrows: "wipe" reveals the arrow, while "peek in" pushes it.

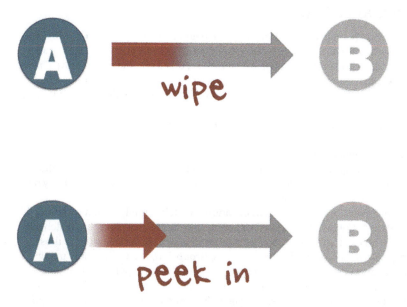

Figure 6-1. *Difference between "wipe" and "peek in"*

"Wipe" implies no movement, and could be replaced by a transition, assuming no delay issue and no other move on the slide. "Peek in" brings the arrow into position, starting from slightly behind the final place reached by the arrow.

Can we use them indifferently? Sometimes, but in most cases it will be one and not the other – when for instance I want to display a scribbled arrow and a short annotation, I "wipe" the arrow from tail to head, then I "wipe" the annotation from left to right because I simulate handwriting and that's how I write. The "peek in" animation wouldn't work. If I were to show a floor lamp coming out of Mary Poppins's carpet bag, I could only use "peek in" because I should see the lamp moving up.

Even when the case looks rather indifferent, as in Figure 6-1, different animations carry a different undertone. "Wipe" reveals an existing connection in Figure 6-1 between A and B. "Peek in," that's at least how I feel it, establishes a far stronger causality between A and B; A implies B, and there is no way to escape it. In the same way that in a sentence a change of preposition can give a different meaning, there is, I believe, a different meaning associated with each animation, a kind of grammar of animations. There are indifferent cases, but there are also many times when one animation illustrates your talk and your meaning better than another one. Once again, the goal isn't to wow your audience with cool effects, the goal is that visuals sustain and reinforce what you have to say. I have seen lines of text appearing in a presentation with a "peek in" from bottom (the default direction with many animations); I find the animation annoying because for me it's unnatural. An annoying animation distracts the audience for a fraction of a second and breaks the connection that you are trying to establish with people listening to you. If you want to make text appear, a brisk appearance works, a fade works, a wipe in the direction of writing works, as well as a few other options, but for me it's not what "peek in" should be used for, unless perhaps the movement follows the writing direction. As annoying as "peek in" from bottom is, at least it's not the complete nonsense that would be a "wipe" *opposite* to the direction of writing. As you can guess, I'm not a fan of fancy animations.

I'll try in this chapter first to review the most useful animations. I'll try to give "grammar rules," with examples of application. All grammar rules, of course, have exceptions. There are many animations I have never used.

Appearance/Disappearance Effects

Appearance and disappearance effects (which, I remind you, are called entrance/exit effects in PowerPoint jargon) are in their vast majority symmetrical one of each other; therefore I'll mostly talk about appearance. I'd like to underline that in this category you find two subcategories: those that make the object move ("peek in" was a good example); and those that don't (like "wipe"), which are usually equivalent to a transition. I say "usually" because, we have seen it in the previous chapter; "dissolve" for instance isn't visually the same with animations and transitions.

You can use all animations with either text or graphical elements; options may differ though with appearance/disappearance effects depending on your animating text, SmartArt (you know how I feel about it), or pictures. Pictures are atomic elements. Text is made of letters, words, and paragraphs (and SmartArt is made of various graphical elements). When an object is made of several elements, applying an animation to the object applies the same animation to all its subcomponents; however, the animation can optionally be triggered by one different click for each subcomponent.

Depending on your version of PowerPoint, you'll find in the animation tab something that can be called anything like "Animation Pane," "Custom Animation," or a more cryptic "Reorder" button, which will allow you to see, when you select a piece of text and associate an animation with it, options such as those displayed in Figure 6-2. The drop-down menu with the most options, *Group Text*, lets you say how many times you want to click to animate the text block: once – once per paragraph, or once per subparagraph. Although it's probably one of the first "advanced features" discovered by people starting with animations, I find it mostly useless: first, you should *not* have a lot of text on your slides, and five sublevels of paragraphs is something I would definitely not recommend. Second, it's far more convenient, unless you are totally addicted to copy/paste, to have as many different text boxes as you have pieces of text to animate; it gives you more freedom with the layout, and you can associate, if needed, different types of animation with each different text box (I remind you that with *Group Text* every piece is animated in the same way). *Animate Text* refers to what happens after a click: whether the "group" will be animated as one chunk, by word, or by letter. I find animation by word useless, but animating by letter can be quite useful for simulating typing or handwriting, as I'm going to discuss shortly. I have never used any of the other options in the "Text Animations" pane. I should however mention something I use from time to time, especially with text, and that you find under "Effect Options": dimming after animation.

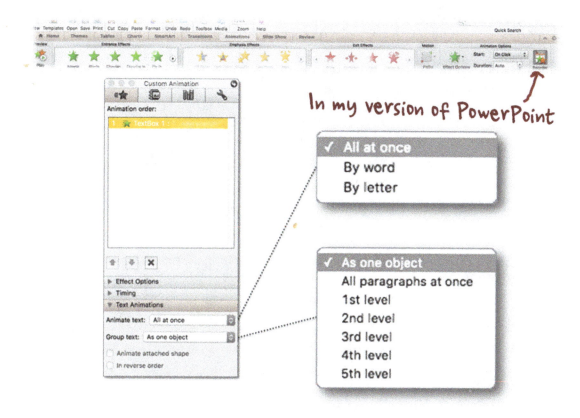

Figure 6-2. *Special options when animating text*

Appearance effects are roughly as numerous as transitions, and as with transitions very few are really useful. Figure 6-3 shows the appearance effects I'm using all the time (once again, your version of PowerPoint may show a different list, and some of them may be listed under "More Entrance Effects" or similar); among these I've highlighted in yellow those more important to my eyes, and in blue those that I could live without. In my opinion, you should exert utter caution before using anything else.

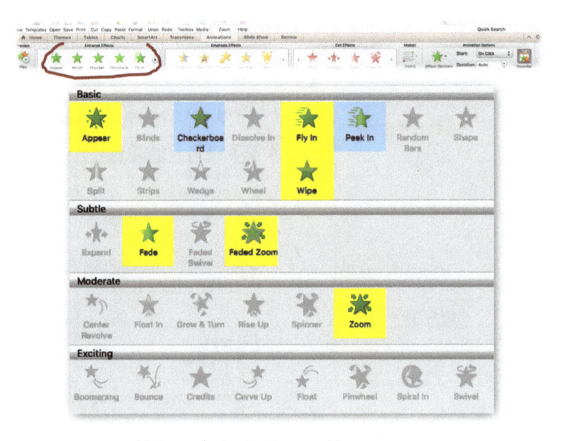

Figure 6-3. *Appearance (aka Entrance) animations that are useful*

As promised, here are my grammar rules:

Appear

The object becomes visible on click. Implications are neutral.

Moving object: No – visually the same as no transition or "Cut" transition.

Usage: Useful for following a different movement, such as making appear an object pointed to by an animated arrow. In a combination of various animations, if you want to see an object brutally appear after a wiped arrow as in Figure 6-1, for instance, I find using the animation more convenient than a transition to a different slide.

Checkerboard

The object is revealed through a checkerboard pattern.

Moving object: No – however, not quite the same as the similarly named transition that isn't idempotent and reveals a black background (animations don't affect the background).

Usage: I use it for only one purpose: with the option "By letter" for "Animate Text" (important), it simulates typing extremely well, in fact almost better than the "typewriter" animation available in some versions of PowerPoint.

Fly In

The object comes in place following a straight line from the outside of the slide, crossing the slide edge (it can also come across a slide corner).

Moving object: Yes.

Usage: That's what you use to introduce something important and remarkable, such as text or a new image illustrating a concept: the actor enters the stage. You shouldn't use it too often for the same "actor" though, unless your audience has seen the actor explicitly "leaving the stage." "Fly in" can also be used to represent the external world bursting into the presentation, under the guise of a mouse cursor for instance.

Peek In

The object comes in place from one of its edges (or near one of it's edges), as if it were pulled from under the rug.

Moving object: Yes.

Usage: It can be used for a number of cases:

- With arrows, strong implication or causality as already shown.

- It can also reveal something that is already latent; for instance, when displaying a hierarchy of directories on a computer you can display a first level of directories then, peeking in from top, a sublevel of directories. The subdirectories were supposed to already be in the directories, no need for a "fly in" grand entrance. At the same time, the animation carries a better feeling of drilling down than "appear," which is also usable.

- It's a "jack-in-the-box" animation, which you can use whenever something is supposed to project out of something else (while remaining on the slide).

Wipe

The object is revealed, from the selected side.

Moving object: No. It can be replaced by the similarly named transition in a number of cases.

Usage: Applied in the writing direction, it's very good for simulating writing or typing for a *single* line of text (for several lines, use "Fade" with script fonts and "Checkerboard" with other fonts). With images, there is with "wipe" an even stronger idea of latency than with "peek in": a revealed object was already here, hidden. In many cases, you'll have to choose between "wipe" and "peek in"; for instance, the directory example I gave with "peek in" also works with a "wipe from top." "Wipe" is simply a little less dynamic. Choosing between the two often depends on concurrent animations. You can also use the "wipe" animation with images that cover the whole surface of the slide. I gave in the preceding chapter the example of an "intermission" slide with a falling curtain; a curtain image could as well be wiped from top to cover a slide, and, after the intermission, removed with the matching disappearance effect.

Fade

The object slowly appears.

Moving object: No. It can be replaced by the similarly named transition in many cases.

Usage: "Fade" is to animations (and transitions) what gray or black is to your wardrobe: you can mix it with almost anything without fearing a blunder. When you have several lines of annotations to display, "fade" associated with the option "By letter" for "Animate Text" simulates cursive writing rather well. For other cases, "fade," like "wipe," has a very strong connotation of latency. "Fade" is slightly more static than "wipe."

Faded Zoom (sometimes called "Zoom")

It's, as the name implies, a combination of fading and zooming. Note that it's always a zoom in, which means that the object grows from nothing (in my version of PowerPoint, but fading doesn't make too much sense in a zoom out). Zooms have an interesting feature: they introduce a third dimension (depth).

Moving object: Yes. It conveys a feeling of motion perpendicularly to the slide surface.

Usage: Bringing the focus on something already on the screen. The discussion of a particular item in a menu is a good example: suppose that you have on screen a snapshot of the Gimp toolbox, and want to discuss one particular tool. Extract the tool icon from the toolbox, make it bigger through scaling (as big as you can without getting something blurry), place the big icon over the small one in the toolbox, and use a faded zoom to make it appear (adding a shadow to the big icon will reinforce the depth feeling).

Zoom (sometimes called "Basic Zoom")

Make the object grow from nowhere (zoom in), or shrink in place from nowhere (zoom out).

Moving object: Yes. It conveys a feeling of motion perpendicularly to the slide surface.

Usage: "Zoom in" is a slightly harsher version of "faded zoom." "Zoom out" brings in an interesting twist, a feeling of transcendence – something not only coming from the outside, but from *above*, not unlike the ironic voice of the author in some novels. For text, it looks like a rubber stamp, and it can reinforce a very important message. If you want to show interaction with a touchscreen, it's a stronger way to introduce the picture of a hand than "fly in." A moderate usage can turn "zoom out" into a strong stress on what matters.

I find most of the other *entrance* effects useless; I'm more indulgent with disappearance effects, but only when they are matching my talk, such as "drop" to illustrate that something is ignored. I'm trying to stick to this rule for fancy effects: if the name of the effect matches a word I plan to say, I use the effect and trigger it when I say the word. So far I have never managed to get "boomerang" in edgewise.

Emphasis Effects

Emphasis effects only change the looks of an object that was there before the effect kicked in; the object will still be there when the effect completes, but either it will look different from what it was or it will have looked different for a moment. As applying emphasis to a lot of objects on the same slide would be self-defeating, emphasis usually concerns a single object, and many effects that merely alter colors are in my opinion better and more easily rendered by using two successive slides with the object colored differently, and an idempotent transition between the two slides. Besides, the numerous idempotent transitions give you more options for switching from one state to the other.

Beware that emphasis effects that result in a move or change of size of the object are set in a way that differs very significantly from what happens when you define an appearance effect: when you associate an appearance effect with an object, what you see on your screen while you prepare your presentation is the object as it will look and where it will be when the animation has completed. With emphasis effects, as with disappearance effects (and motions paths that you'll soon see), what you see on your screen is the object as it appears *before* the animation starts. It makes a very big difference when you are chaining slides in a sequence. With a disappearance effect, there is no problem: you know that on the next slide the object will be gone. With other animations, on the next slide the object will still be there, but after the animation it will look different or be at another place. If you want any continuity the object should look on the next slide like it will appear after the animation, and be precisely positioned where the animation will take it on the current slide. I have tried to show in Figure 6-4 what you must do if you want to shrink the image of an elephant in a sequence (as an aside, percentages by which you grow or shrink objects refer to by how much you grow or shrink each dimension; if you divide width and height by two, the resulting image is actually four times smaller). If image-formatting options let you reduce the size very precisely for the second slide, the difficulty is with positioning the smaller image exactly where the "shrink" animation takes the bigger image on the first slide. There are, in PowerPoint, tools for aligning objects, but their point of reference is the slide, not an object in the slide. Either you use a calculator and try to compute very precisely what should be the position values in "Format Image"; or you run the slideshow starting from the first slide and use up and down arrows to switch between the second slide and the first slide after the move, trying to estimate how position should be adjusted, and then set it manually (this is what I usually do, but it's one of those things that become easier with practice). A faded transition will eliminate any unpleasant visual jump if the position is wrong by one pixel or two.

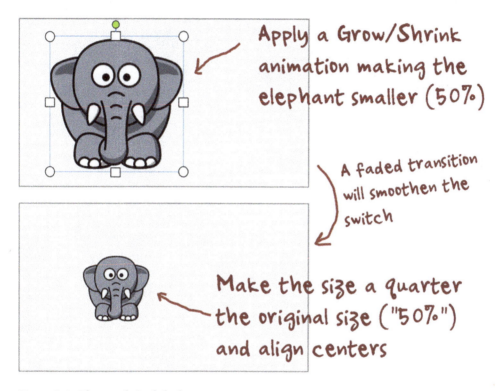

Figure 6-4. *The travel-sized elephant*

You haven't this problem if the emphasis effect is applied on the *last* slide of a sequence, before switching to something different. If your purpose really is emphasis, the last slide is usually where you want emphasis to be. When you shrink objects, though, it's not what you can call emphasis, and you usually shrink objects to make room before continuing the sequence. Be aware if you have a very tight deadline that slide continuity after emphasis may require extra work.

I have shown in Figure 6-5, as I did in Figure 6-3 with appearance/disappearance effects, the emphasis effects I find useful. I only commonly use "Grow/Shrink" and "Spin"; "Spin" can actually be used for many rotations, which with experience occur more often in presentations than you would think.

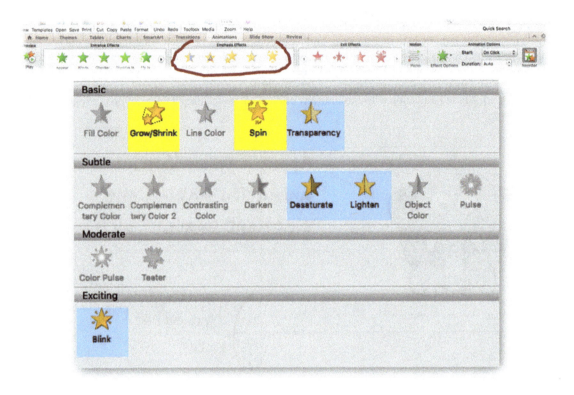

Figure 6-5. *Emphasis animations that are useful*

Let's briefly review the most useful emphasis effect one by one.

Grow/Shrink

Make an object (usually a picture) bigger or smaller. Some PowerPoint versions allow you to specify an arbitrary percentage, but other versions don't. Beware that growing an object too big may make it blurry.

Moving object: Yes, even if it's not in the usual sense of "motion." It cannot be replaced by a transition.

Usage: "Grow" can be used as an alternative in the same way (but with only one image) if you want to put the focus on one independent element in the slide. "Shrink" is probably more interesting because it allows you to show something at a size that is legible even for people at the back of the room, then make it far smaller to make room for something else *while keeping the object on the slide* and retaining "the big picture," even if once shrunk it's no longer legible. As previously said, expect a bit of work on continuity.

If you want to grow or shrink text or shapes that contain text, right-click on the object and select "Format Text" or "Format Shape," and make sure that in the "text box" submenu the "Autofit" option is set to "Resize text to fit shape"; otherwise the font size won't change.

Spin

Make an object rotate, clockwise or counterclockwise. Some PowerPoint versions allow specifying an arbitrary number of degrees; other versions don't and have a number of preset rotations.

Moving object: Yes.

Usage: Needless to say, if the subject of your talk has any remote connection with mechanics, it's very likely that you'll have to show rotations at one point. On a metaphorical and more general level, rotating cogs express any kind of process very well (I know, it's a bit cliché), and a needle rotating over a dial can be handy when talking about performance, among other topics.

Beware that spin rotates the object around its center, which isn't what you want for a needle. The solution for spinning around a different axis is illustrated in Figure 6-6: apply the "spin" effect to a compound object made of the object that you want to rotate grouped with a transparent rectangle (obviously not completely transparent in the figure). I already mentioned grouping at the end of Chapter 3; you group objects by left-clicking on multiple objects while keeping the "Shift" key down (it allows multiple selections), then by right-clicking and selecting "Group." A group can be grouped with other objects.

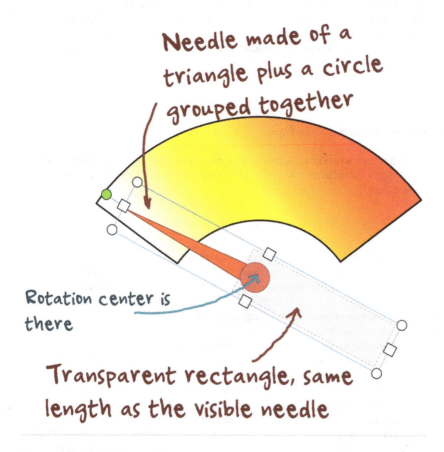

Figure 6-6. Rotating a needle

The transparent rectangle has to be placed so that the axis is spot in the middle of the visible and invisible parts together. As working with transparent objects is a bit difficult, you should draw a rectangle the size of the original object, format it with a visible border and the "Fill" property set to "None," place it, group, click on the group to select it, click a second time on the rectangle within the group, and then set its border property to "None" when you are sure that everything is in the right position (elements in a group can be independently modified and even moved around).

Transparency, Desaturate, Lighten

Those three "emphasis" effects (de-emphasis effects might be more appropriate), which very often are hard to tell from one another on a slide, respectively make an object diaphanous, turn it to tones of gray, or lighten its colors.

Moving object: No.

Usage: The purpose is the same with all three effects: dimming an object so that the attention of the audience can focus on something else. I remind you that most animations have a "dim after animation" option that serves the same purpose but simply changes the color of the object. These effects are better alternatives with images (shapes, cliparts, photographs). I have said in Chapter 3 how much I like, for multiple reasons, to replace a live demo with simulated action against a user-interface re-created with shapes; very briefly applied to a rectangle representing a button, "transparency" or "lighten" looks very much like a click.

Blink

Makes the object disappear and appear very quickly. The effect can be repeated.

Moving object: No.

Usage: A blinking object on a screen requires attention in an almost embarrassing way; however I use "blink" (pretty regularly) for blinking a cursor image over a button (combined with "transparency" for the button) when I want to indicate a click.

Motion Effects

No motion effect can be replaced with a transition: their purpose is to move an object from one place to another on one slide (some effects are closed-loop motions, but I have never found use for any of them); "on one slide" isn't to be taken too literally, because nothing prevents from starting or ending a motion (or both) *outside* the visible scope of a slide. As a consequence, the "fly in" entrance or disappearance effect is nothing more than a linear motion effect. I have mentioned the only significant difference when talking about emphasis effects, whereas an entrance effect *brings* an object to the position where you place it, a motion effect, by default, *takes* an object from the position where you place it (there is, however, the possibility of reversing a motion path, an option available when you right-click on it). The continuity problem I have underlined with "shrink" when a slide follows in the sequence also exists with motion paths.

Another point to take care of with any animation that moves the object, an almost systematic concern with motion paths, is what I have mentioned at the end of Chapter 3: every new object is created in a new plane in a stack, and motion always takes place within one plane. You need to define precisely where objects are supposed to be placed between foreground and background, and stack them accordingly. I have illustrated a move within a plane in Figure 6-7, using the same example already seen at the end of Chapter 3: we want to represent the storage of a value into a named place in memory (a variable), but this time we are adding a motion. The motion really makes sense here, because when I say that I store value 42 at the place known as "my_variable," value 42 doesn't appear all of a sudden, we *store* it into the variable. It's the result of an action, a move. As I don't want to be too specific about how the value came into the computer in the first place (it might have been typed in, it might have arrived through a network, it might have been computed...) I make the value start from outside the slide, and a curved path brings it *between* the background of the box and the foreground, thus giving the illusion of being put into the box.

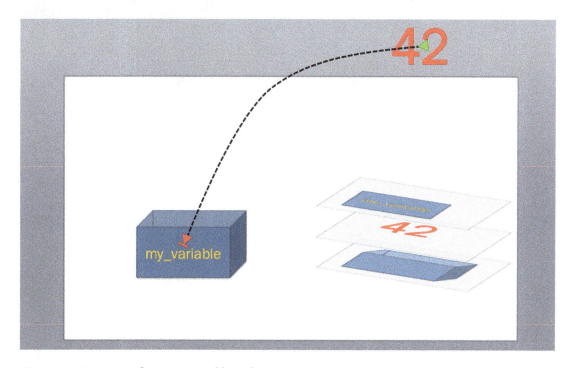

Figure 6-7. *Storing a value into a variable, with motion*

At the end of its course, the value looks *in* the box. Whenever I explain the logic of a program, I usually show these "boxes" by the code, and show how values change as I step into the code.

As I have done with other animations, I have shown in Figure 6-8 the motion paths that are useful – in my view, only the "custom" ones, those for which you define both the starting *and* the ending point. "Basic" motion paths let you click to define a starting point, and have a preset ending point that you can change, but then I don't see much difference between "custom" and "basic." Although I can't exclude having to use a closed-loop move one day, I have never found any practical use for them: if you have to explain a cycle (thermodynamics, for instance, or whatever you can think of – even moving a car clipart over a map to explain a travel itinerary), it's very likely that when you are going to talk you won't explain everything in one go, but you are going to have a motion up to one point in the cycle, explain, then a motion from there to another point, explain, and so forth until you close the loop. You'll need as many clicks as you have legs in the cycle; a closed-loop motion is a one-click operation. Remember that motions aren't gratuitous, but are there to support your talk; it's not "let's move everything on the screen then explain" – motion and speech must be linked.

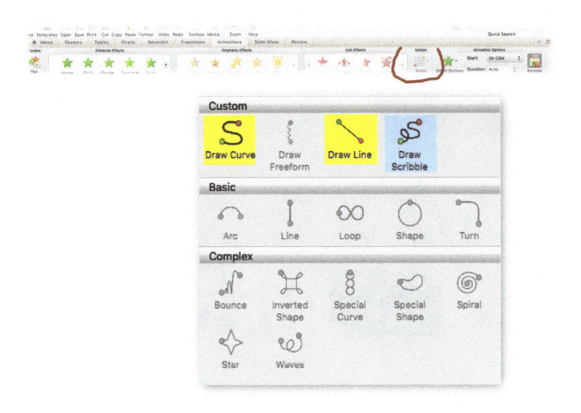

Figure 6-8. *Useful motion paths*

A curved path is what I have used in Figure 6-7 when storing the value inside the box, and I use very often lines as well. The "scribble" path may in some cases be useful if you have to move an object alongside a complex path, for instance, for representing a flow of material when animating a schema.

Motion paths are extremely fickle. Sometimes you select a starting point and an ending point, and you end up with a path that is parallel to what you defined but shifted, and that takes your element to a different place from the one that was intended. It can be frustrating at times. Sometimes you can modify the path and bring it where it should be (but modifying paths isn't easy); sometimes starting from a different point in your element works like a charm. Don't hesitate to start from the opposite corner, or from the center, or from an edge, and keep your fingers crossed.

In my version of PowerPoint, whenever I create a motion animation I have two "effect options" settings, *Smooth Start* and *Smooth End*, which are enabled by default. In some versions of PowerPoint they are enabled through check boxes, other versions use sliders that should be set to zero. The default settings of appearance effects such as "fly in," which also supports these options, are different. I find these settings most annoying, and I usually disable all fancy options. *Smooth* is PowerPoint jargon for acceleration/deceleration. I'll talk in the next pages about combining animations; when you combine animations any acceleration or deceleration turns a move into something that is very difficult to control precisely. I guess that the purpose of these settings is to give more realism to moves, but my opinion here is the same one I have expressed when talking in Chapter 3 about sketching user interfaces: my concern is clarity, not realism. Besides, I don't see why a block of text or a shape moving across the screen should be submitted to the laws of physics.

As a side note, when you move an image onscreen it's not necessarily a static image: you can displace an animated .gif file. Animated .gif files can be created using Gimp, applying the old principle of cartoons: slightly different layers that are displayed in quick succession. They can in some cases make an animated schema more interesting. As always, don't overdo it.

Timing

I have said at the beginning of this chapter that animations allow far more precise timing than transitions. When defining a transition, you can set how long the transition will take, and you can also say for fugitive slides that the switch to the next slide will occur automatically, as soon as every animation has run its course or after a delay. With animations, you can set the duration, as well as define when the animation is triggered, which is very important when you have several animations on one slide.

Duration

I wish to point out that presentation software (it's the same story in PowerPoint and in LibreOffice Impress) has a definition of speed that doesn't quite match what I have been taught at school, a long time ago. As you can see in Figure 6-9, there are at places correct references to "Duration" and elsewhere references to "Speed." Speed, in my world, has never been expressed in seconds. Saying that 0.5 s is "Very Fast" demands some qualification; if you move by one inch in half a second, that's about 0.11 mph (0.18 km/h); a Galapagos tortoise, which races at almost twice that speed, would leave you far behind. Speed, for what I know, is a ratio of distance to time.

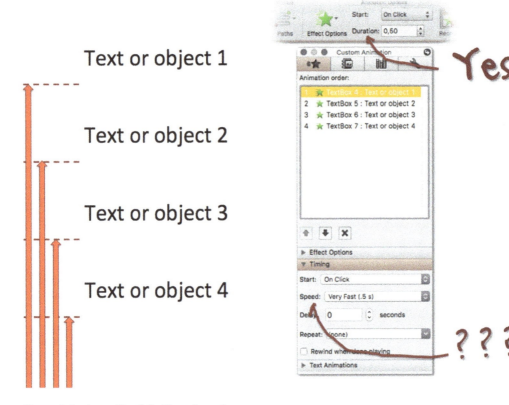

Figure 6-9. *A peculiar definition of speed*

You might think I'm splitting hair. In fact, a correct definition of speed is far more important than it seems. Suppose that, as on the left-hand side in Figure 6-9, I have four different objects that I want to make appear with a "fly in" entrance effect. If I keep all options by default, the direction will be from bottom, and the "speed," PowerPoint-style, will be "Very Fast," or 0.5 s for every object. You might expect that all four elements will appear in exactly the same way, which is untrue: the first element will travel four times the distance traveled by the last one, during the same amount of time. In other words, the element at the bottom will move up four times slower than the one at the top. It may not be obvious to you when you rehearse your presentation on your laptop, but it may be more obvious to your audience when projected on a large screen, with elements not closer than one foot from each other.

If your elements are displayed from top to bottom, as might be expected, visual speed will decrease as you progress in your talk. Speed is usually associated with excitement. Conversely, slowing down will bring a feeling of growing boredom that may just sit below the level of conscious perception. Like it or not, as a speaker you are a performer; slowing down puts you in the position of a circus artist who starts a number with the most exciting demonstrations of skills, and ends up with easier and easier feats. Circus performers know better.

In the same way, if you want to animate with a "wipe" animation rectangles representing bars in a chart, displaying every bar, irrespective of its length, in the same time will reinforce your message if the longer the bar, the better (revenues, throughput), because what will move fastest on screen will be what is best. It will contradict your message if the shorter the bar, the better (costs, resources consumption).

You have several solutions: with a chart, if displaying all bars at once is acceptable, you should consider a "wipe" transition (idempotent) rather than animations. Generally speaking, you can also get your calculator and set the duration of each move to a value that is proportional to the distance traveled to keep speed constant (my definition of speed). With text as in Figure 6-9, if you are as lazy as I am, the easy option is to change the direction of entrance and make objects enter sideways, from the left: unless the text length varies wildly, a rare case, you'll get almost uniform speed. Finally, I'd like to remind you of a technique that I have already mentioned in Chapter 2: you can rekindle interest by creating a break and changing the motion direction unexpectedly. For instance, in Figure 6-9 you could make enter elements one to three sideways, and the last one from the bottom – or the reverse.

Triggering

By default, an animation is triggered by a click, and you only switch to the next slide when all animations have fired. You can also specify that an animation starts at the same time as the preceding one or after the preceding one has completed, in both cases with or without a delay. In practice, delays are mostly useful with the "appear" (or "disappear") animation, the duration of which is zero; without a delay, starting another animation after it is exactly the same as starting it at the same time. A delay reintroduces a sense of sequence.

Some versions of PowerPoint feature a graphical time timeline where you can drag starting and ending times, as well as the whole movement respectively to other movements, a tool that is most convenient. Where it's missing, you can reorder effects using arrows and type in the times.

When and how to trigger animations is better explained through examples; a few follow, and I'll give many more in the next chapter.

Combinations

If you can animate several elements on your screen at the same time, you can also apply several animations at once to the same element. You usually combine animations from different categories. Some predefined animations are already compound animations: for instance, a faded zoom is a faded appearance effect starting at the same time as a zoom effect (two appearance effects combined, a highly unusual combination). By combining animations, usually of different types (entrance and emphasis, or emphasis and motion), you can obtain very interesting visual illustrations. I'm going to give two practical examples that combine appearance and motion, then emphasis and motion.

Appearance and Motion: Slanted Zoom

I have mentioned when talking about appearance effects that a faded zoom was quite suitable for bringing the focus on a particular tool in the Gimp toolbox. This effect can be even more effective when combined with a linear motion; some zooming options allow these kinds of effects, but with a limited choice of origins. I have illustrated a faded zoom combined with a motion in Figure 6-10. On the left-hand side, I'm using a plain faded zoom. I have isolated the lasso representing the "free select" tool in the Gimp toolbox, and scaled it up so that it's perfectly visible for people at the back. Because a faded zoom will grow this image in place, I have had to keep the light gray background; without the background, the lasso would blend with the other tools in the toolbox and would be hard to see. I have added a thin black border to make my icon cleaner, and a shadow to accentuate the depth effect. It's quite legible even from afar, but because this picture hides a part of the toolbox, we are losing the context: this tool obviously belongs to the set at the top of the toolbox, but its exact location is lost, and the neighboring tools are hidden as well. Users confronted with the Gimp toolbox for the first time after the presentation may have a little difficulty finding their footing. On the right-hand side of Figure 6-10, I'm still using a faded zoom, but I'm combining it with a linear motion that starts "With Previous" and brings the lasso image outside the toolbox. For combining these two animations, I must take care of two points:

Figure 6-10. *Combining motion and faded zoom*

- The durations must be identical. By default, the duration of the faded zoom will be 0.5 seconds, while the duration of the linear motion will be 2 seconds. I must set both to some kind of compromise value, such as 1 second or 1.5 seconds.

- I must disable the *Smooth Start* and *Smooth End* settings for the linear path; otherwise the resulting move will look weird.

The linear side motion may look a small detail, but it brings several benefits: as I can move my icon to a location where it will contrast with the background on the slide, the animated image no longer needs to have a background of its own; I have made its background transparent. My icon is less bulky, and additionally I have been able to increase the contrast of the lasso, making it far more visible (I also have slightly increased the contrast on the left-hand side, but I didn't want the gray background to turn white). Now, the audience can still see the context when the icon is magnified.

Emphasis and Motion: The Big Picture

We can now deal with the question I had left unanswered at the end of Chapter 5: if we present the nuclear waste management diagram as a virtual schema that spreads outside the surface of one slide, is there a way to show the big picture, once we have gone through every component in the schema through "push" transitions taking us from quadrant to quadrant? Yes, and the solution relies on combined animations.

As the schema that is presented through "push" transitions is a virtual one, the first step consists in turning it into a real image using Gimp. I have illustrated the process in Figure 6-11. I have transformed each one of the quadrants into an image; then I took the image corresponding to what I had called quadrant A in chapter 5 (top-left quadrant), which is framed in orange in Figure 6-11. Using the "Image/Canvas Size" option, I have redefined the size of quadrant A as double its original width and double its original height, with the purpose of adding all the other quadrants to quadrant A as indicated by the arrows in the figure. Then I selected all quadrants other than A in turn, copied them, and pasted them as new layers (easier for positioning) into the resized quadrant A image before precisely adjusting all quadrants and exporting the resulting full image as a .png file.

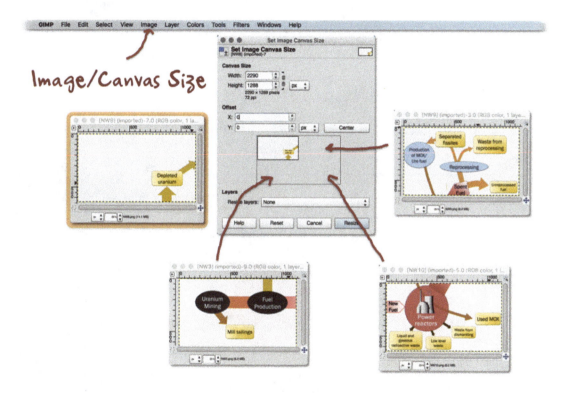

Figure 6-11. *Preparing the big picture*

Having the full image ready, we can now insert it into the presentation; remember, we have seen in the previous chapter that elements, images included, can spill outside the visible area of slides. A simple way of adding the full schema image to the presentation is partly illustrated in Figure 6-12:

- Make the *last* slide before we start showing the big picture the current one. In the nuclear waste management example, it will be the slide that contains the full "quadrant D."

- Then set the zoom view to 50%, insert the big picture, send it to the background, and increase the size of the picture by dragging its upper-left corner up and leftwards until the elements on the slide exactly cover the relevant part of the big picture; it will be easier if you set the zoom settings to a large value, such as 200%, for final adjustments.

- Insert a new empty slide after the current one, cut the correctly positioned big picture, and paste it on the new slide.

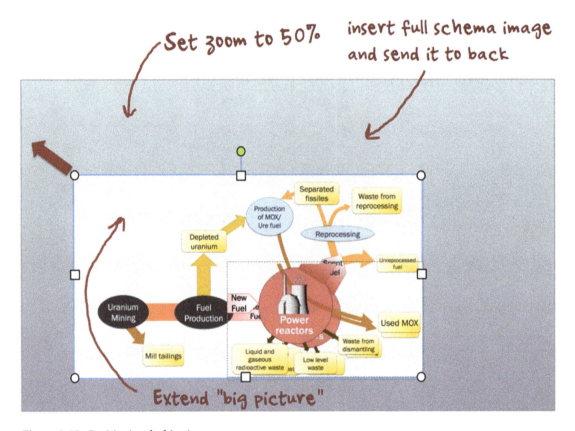

Figure 6-12. *Positioning the big picture*

When running the slideshow, switching from one slide to the next should be unnoticeable.

You can now animate the big picture so that it becomes fully visible, and Figure 6-13 explains the process: what you initially see is the slightly grayed area indicated as "visible slide," which should initially look exactly like the previous slide. You are going to apply to the image the "Grow/Shrink" emphasis effect, changing the options to "Smaller," a 50% reduction applied to both dimensions (the default option is to grow an object). However, by doing so the invariant position in the image will be its center, and if we only shrink the image it will end up at the position shown in the figure by the red dashed frame; we would see the same part of the image, only four times smaller and cornered in the upper-left part of the screen. We need therefore to move the image, which now has the size of the slide, by adding a linear motion that brings the center of the image to the center of the slide. Set shrinking and linear motion to both start "With Previous" (when there is no previous animation, the first animation starts as soon as the slide is displayed, which is exactly what we want here); set both durations to exactly the same value (up to you, something like three seconds would look right to me); disable the *Smooth Start* and *Smooth End* options of the motion path and you are done.

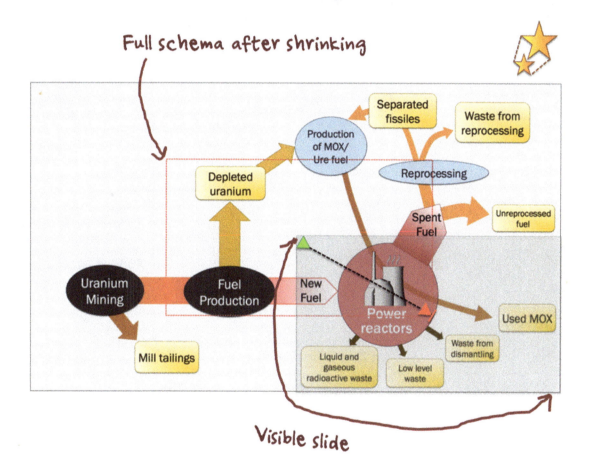

Figure 6-13. *Showing the big picture*

When you advance to the slide, you see a zoom-out effect that reveals the full picture. At that point, the finest print becomes hard to read but it no longer matters as you have already shown it in detail earlier. Now you are ready for a recap and for hammering home your message.

Summary

- Animations allow moves and concurrency that transitions don't allow.

- There should always be a reason for animating an element on a slide.

- You should be careful with duration, and animation timing.

- Several animations can be applied at the same time to the same element.

The real power of projecting to your audience how you picture what you are telling them comes, of course, from combining not only different animations but different techniques and blending them together, as transparently as possible. That will be the topic of the next chapter.

CHAPTER 7

■ ■ ■

Putting the Magic Together

In der Beschränkung zeigt sich erst der Meister.
It is in self-limitation that a master first shows himself.

—Johann Wolfgang von Goethe (1749-1832)

I have in the previous chapters explained a number of techniques to illustrate better what you are talking about. The real difficulty with presentation software, as with any medium, is in overcoming the limitations of the medium to fully express what you want to say; one is always tempted by fitting the presentation to the medium, especially when creating a new slide obligingly suggests "Click to add title" and "Click to add text" (next, in the second case, to a bullet point). In this chapter I am going to discuss a number of text cases showing how to blend animation, transitions, substitutions, and create visual aids that support your talk instead of shaping it: visual aids that no longer look like what they are – a plain PowerPoint presentation. You actually need a surprisingly small number of "effects," none of them particularly fancy, to achieve such a result. I'll put a particular emphasis on fugitive slides to show you how to go from the traditional "next slide" treatment to presentations where, at least in places, you can have a far more fluid and cinematic approach.

Sleight of Hand

Saying that the major part of what you show in a technical presentation is an illusion may look odd. When you think about it, though, whenever you open a technical book, illustrations are mostly schemas and diagrams showing flows of information or flows of material, and present a simplified big picture. Very often in engineering, and software engineering is a case in point, when you show for real how everything "works," the best you can do is show usage, which is significantly different from explaining the underlying principles. It's principles that you want to expose in a presentation or lecture; demonstrations and hands-on labs are dedicated to usage. Explaining fundamentals demands you to enter the territory of imagination and of illusion. When you present, you shouldn't hesitate to let your audience believe that they are seeing something when they are actually looking at something else.

I'm going to illustrate illusion with a first example: presenting set operations. If you are unfamiliar with set operations (which are very important when processing data), they are conceptually rather simple. When you are dealing with two sets of objects, set operations are about finding objects that are common to both sets (these objects constitute what is known as the intersection), objects that belong to either set (the union), and objects that belong to one set but not to the other (the difference, sometimes called complement). To take a simple example, a first set could be "mammals"; another set could be "animals that have fins." Those are two independent sets with a common subset containing marine mammals such as whales or dolphins. Let's use this example in a very short presentation. I'm going to build it little by little, making choices that you should feel free to disagree with – the questions that lead to these choices are important, but the answers only reflect the personal vision of the presenter.

© Stéphane Faroult 2016
S. Faroult, *Getting the Message Across*, DOI 10.1007/978-1-4842-2295-9_7

Figure 7-1 illustrates my answer to the first question: how are we going to represent our sets? The kind of shape that looks best to me is either an ellipse, or a kind of potato (which is the traditional chalk n' blackboard representation of sets). Drawing a potato shape is relatively easy with the "Curve" line-drawing tool of PowerPoint, which you use as the free-select lasso in Gimp, and I chose this type of shape. The question now is the appearance that we want to give to the shapes. Contrasting colors would be a good start. However, if we use plain solid colors, when we want to show that the two sets overlap, the only one that will be shown fully will be that last set drawn, which will be higher in the stack. The audience will guess that there is a common part, but won't see it; additionally, it makes more obvious that we have two different planes, which isn't an idea we want to convey. The solution is to give transparency to the filling color of the "set" on top. I have set in Figure 7-1 transparency to 50% for the yellowish set. Another question we could ask is whether we want to put pictures of animals inside the sets as an illustration. I have chosen to use some, but not immediately: one of my goals is to involve my audience, and, in particular, not to prompt my audience too early with, for instance, pictures of mammals that have fins.

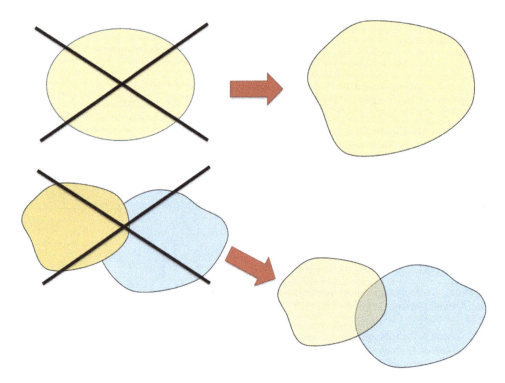

Figure 7-1. *Representing sets*

Once I know what my sets will look like, I must begin to think about the dynamics of my presentation. I have tried to illustrate my thought process in Figure 7-2. Before discussing intersection, union, and the like, I want to show the slide at the bottom of the figure, namely, the set of mammals and the set of animals with fins, with a common area representing mammals with fins. However, if I display this slide all of a sudden it spares, too conveniently, any undue intellectual effort from my audience. I'd rather see them coming by themselves to the idea that both sets have a common part. So, the first slide I'll show will be a single set. Which one? Let's start with mammals. For all sets, I will be grouping the text label and the set shape. Next step, the second set must appear, and then two questions: how, and where? I don't think that a "fly in" entrance from the outside of the slide would really work; when talking about groups of animals, I'm talking about nature and the world that exists. It was there before me, it will still be there after me, and that's a typical case where there should be a very strong idea of latency, with the image emerging into view rather than appearing abruptly from the outside. A fade (either the animation or the transition version, it doesn't really matter) looks to me the best way to introduce the second set. I mentioned a second question though, "where": if the second set appears at the right place, showing that some of the animals with fins are actually mammals, I'm giving up on any opportunity to involve my audience. For this reason, I prefer to start with two disjoint sets. These two sets give me the opportunity to ask whether my representation is correct, to get, hopefully without too much prompting, a resounding "no!" as the answer. Then I'll "correct" my slide by triggering a simultaneous and opposite move of the two sets so as to finally get the slide at the bottom of Figure 7-2.

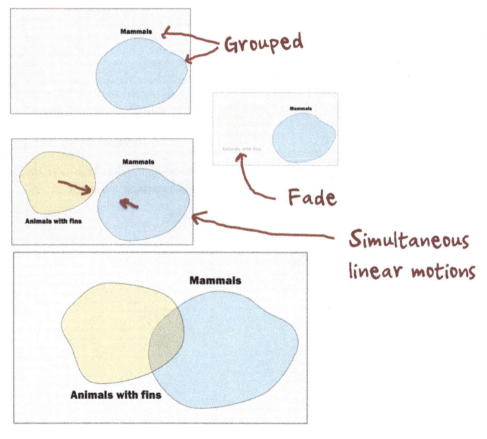

Figure 7-2. Introducing sets

At this stage, two problems appear: the first one is that, even with transparency, the "Animals with fins" potato shape still looks above the "Mammals" potato shape. The telling sign is the part of the outline of the "Mammals" potato shape that is inside the other potato shape: it's yellowish, not as black as the other outlines. The two sets aren't exactly equivalent. Minor problem, but in mathematics, and with operations in particular, symmetry is an important notion; under the name "commutativity" it's the important propriety that the result is the same irrespective of the order of the operands, as with addition, for instance.

The second problem at hand is more serious: I'd like to emphasize separately intersection, difference, and union. During a live presentation, I could try to point out in one way or another (laser pointer, finger, or cursor), but it wouldn't work very well in a large auditorium; and it would work even less in a video. What I'd really want to do is change the color of the area I'm talking about, let's say turn it to a bright yellow. That's a problem for the intersection, because if I can change the fill color of one shape, I cannot do it for a part of a shape, especially an area that is irregular. I could try to draw another shape on top, but it would be very hard by hand. Even the union is a problem: if I change the fill color of both shapes to a bright yellow, it can no longer be transparent for any set because otherwise I'd see differences of shades, when I want everything in a uniform color; without transparency, I'll have an outline issue.

I can solve both these problems with a sleight of hands: I was working with shapes, I'm going to substitute to them an image. I prepared a slide with the two sets in the final position as shown at the bottom of Figure 7-2; placing the objects exactly where motion takes them is the most delicate phase. Then, I have set the zooming factor in PowerPoint to 200%, and taken a screenshot. This 200% factor is very convenient, because it improves resolution and I know that if I later adjust the size of the image down to 50% with the image formatting options, it will be exactly the size of the original object. I have then processed my screenshot as shown in Figure 7-3: using Gimp, I first removed the background, and then I duplicated the layer to be able to create a pure, black outline. I first used the "color to alpha" transform with each one of the three large colored areas in the new layer.

When turning several colors to alpha one after the other, process last "pure" saturated colors (which include white and black). Composite colors in which pure colors have been turned to transparent are difficult to deal with, as the color picker doesn't always pick what you'd want.

Then I desaturated (using "Colors/Desaturate") this layer to turn any hint of yellow to gray. I duplicated the layer and merged it back, plus some play on brightness and contrast, so as to finally obtain a clean, uniform black outline on a transparent layer.

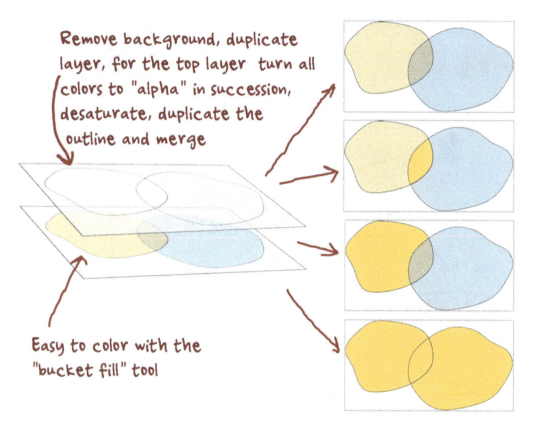

Remove background, duplicate layer, for the top layer turn all colors to "alpha" in succession, desaturate, duplicate the outline and merge

Easy to color with the "bucket fill" tool

Figure 7-3. *Processing the screenshot*

From the two-layered image represented on the left-hand side of Figure 7-3, I generated the four images on the right-hand side: first, at the top, an image very similar to the original screenshot, but with the uniform black outline added; it removes the "yellow over blue" feeling. Then I duplicated the two-layered image three times and used the "bucket-fill" tool (the icon of which represents paint poured out of a can) to color each area on which I want to focus.

With these four images, I'm ready to create my sequence, and the detail is shown in Figure 7-4 (I have omitted the faded appearance of the second set shown in Figure 7-2). My sequence is animated by four clicks, but I have six slides: one of them is a fugitive slide. In Figure 7-2, my click was activating the motion of the two sets toward each other. However, at the end of the move, I don't want to see my two shapes at their final position, with a yellowish outline where the yellow set covers the blue one. I want to see my edited screenshot, with a uniformly black outline. I need a fugitive slide that will automatically transition to my image (top right in Figure 7-4), which will appear with a fade.

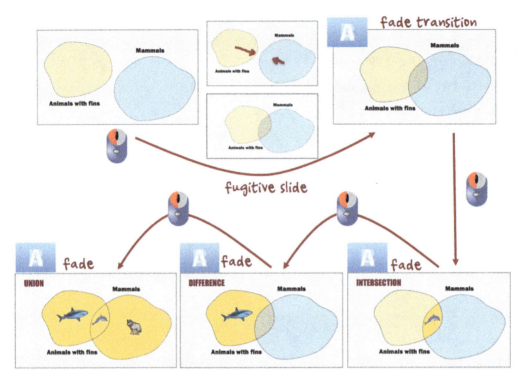

Figure 7-4. *Set operations, remainder of the sequence*

You cannot trigger animations by clicking on a fugitive slide: everything fires automatically. Therefore I have changed tack. There is no animation at all on my slide with the two disjoint sets (top left in Figure 7-4). Animations start automatically in the fugitive slide, and you see in the middle at the top of Figure 7-4 what the slide looks like when animation starts, and what it looks like when animation ends, just before switching imperceptibly to the image with a fade. This image must be exactly positioned. Then I have a succession of fade transitions to display the various images with different highlights (I have also added cliparts to make my presentation less abstract); as all the images were created from the same source, they just need to have exactly the same size and the same coordinates on the screen, and continuity will be flawless.

Substituting a screenshot to a combination of shapes is a technique I'm very fond of, because there are tons of modifications that you can apply to images but cannot apply to other elements (coloring as you have just seen is an excellent example); in fact, I sometimes even take screenshots of text, when I plan to grow or shrink it. It's also the type of stealthy effect that avoids any break in your narrative; nobody will see it if you do it well, but it will sustain efficiently your presentation.

The Computer Code Sawn in Half

Keeping a visual continuity in a sequence seems to me a crucial point for keeping the interest of the audience. I often use animations for shifting elements from one place to another place that is more suitable for what I'll present next, and I'm going to give you a programming example (in the Python programming language, if it matters); the example doesn't require any programming knowledge to be understood.

Figure 7-5 presents my test case. The colors mimic how a text editor used by a programmer would display the text (the text editor recognizes words that have a special meaning in the language as well as constants, and gives them different colors). In the slide at the top I have a program snippet that prompts for the numerator and the denominator of a fraction and reads their values into two variables, then computes the ratio before displaying it; blue lines starting with a pound sign (#) are comments in the code that are ignored by the computer. This example is a very naive example of programming, which works right under suitable conditions but crashes inelegantly when input isn't as expected. For instance, this program would crash with the kind of error message that scares an end user if zero were input as the value for the denominator (the value by which we divide); the result of a run where zero is input could be shown at the bottom of the slide during the presentation.

The slide at the bottom presents one way of handling the specific issue of a user trying to divide by zero: adding an **if** statement that checks whether the denominator is indeed different from zero. When it's zero, the case is handled by the **else** part of the code, which displays a user-friendly message. The bottom slide is in fact a slightly revamped version of the top slide: I have added in Figure 7-5 a yellow dashed box around a few computer instructions that will stay at the very same place in the two slides, and a blue dashed box around a few instructions that don't change but appear at different places (these dashed boxes would not normally appear on the slides). There are also a few additional instructions in the bottom slide.

To present the top slide, I would display the code bit by bit, first showing what is in the dashed yellow box, using probably the "checkerboard" animation with the "by letter" option to simulate typing; then I would display the comment that says "divide" and the instruction that computes the ratio as the second step, then the instruction that displays the result as the third one. I would probably also show what a run would look like with acceptable values before raising the problem of what happens when the second value entered is zero. Now, my problem is to switch from the top slide to the bottom slide. One solution might be to rely on what I have in the dashed yellow box to maintain continuity, and chain both slides either with no transition (cut), a fade, or a wipe from top. It's definitely a solution I would contemplate if I were short on time. We can, however, do better.

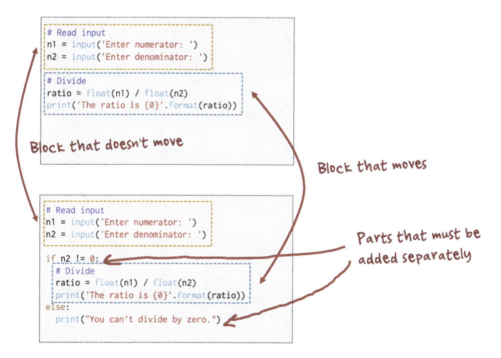

Figure 7-5. *Start and end slides*

Using a transition has three weaknesses:

- If the link between the two slides is perfectly obvious for the block of instructions that doesn't move, it may not be as clear with the block that moves for those people in the audience who aren't gifted with a photographic memory or simply had a moment of absence. Your audience will not see the two slides next to each other as in Figure 7-5, but one after the other, and looking for resemblances and differences requires some effort.

- If you want to display the new instructions piece by piece, as would be logical if that's what you did earlier, the second slide will initially be only composed of the same elements as the first one, except that the block that moves will jump to its new position. A jump is visually unpleasant, and the difference of positions is too important for a fade to smoothen the move.

- The slides don't really represent what a programmer would do to modify the code: opening the code in a text editor, inserting lines and spaces or tabs, and typing additional instructions.

It's better to use animations to bring the audience imperceptibly from one slide to the other, moving blocks of code on the screen. It won't really simulate work in a text editor, but the representation will be far closer to what a developer would do.

Figure 7-6 shows the first steps to take to prepare a smooth passage from one slide to the next. Firstly, I have duplicated the first slide twice: in step 1, I have changed the font color in the first duplicate to a relatively unobtrusive color such as gray or brown.

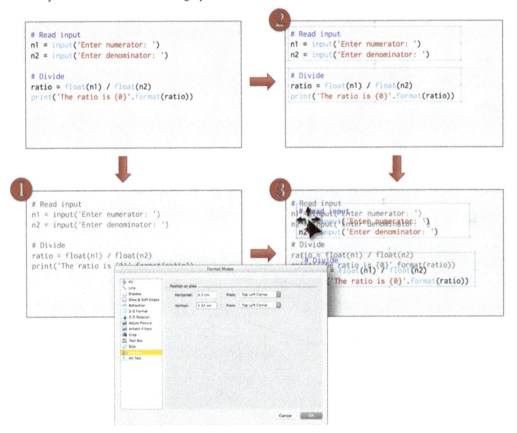

Figure 7-6. *Splitting the original code*

This copy of the original slide is used as a template for positioning text; a template is just a single regular block of text that I'll use to set the position of several smaller sub-blocks of text, and that I'll delete when no longer needed. In step 2, I have in my second duplicate separated the program text into two distinct blocks, the block that won't move and the block that will. As the process of creating those two separate blocks – copy, paste, remove unwanted text - usually leads to displacing them, I have selected them both, cut them, and pasted them in step 3 on my template with gray text. The next operation consists in aligning precisely the blocks of text over the gray template. First drag with the mouse in the neighborhood of the target position, then set zooming to a large value, select the piece of text to place, right-click, and adjust position under "Format Shape" (or whatever your presentation software features for that purpose). Once blocks of text are correctly and precisely positioned, you can remove the gray template.

An important feature of presentation software is that when you copy an element from a slide onto another slide, the position of the element on the second slide will be exactly the same as on the original slide, unless this position conflicts with an element that is already present (in which case the pasted object will be slightly shifted). I'm using this feature very often, and you see it in action in Figure 7-7: after having created a template for the second slide in exactly the same way as I did for the first slide, I copied the two elements over this template; both blocks keep their original position.

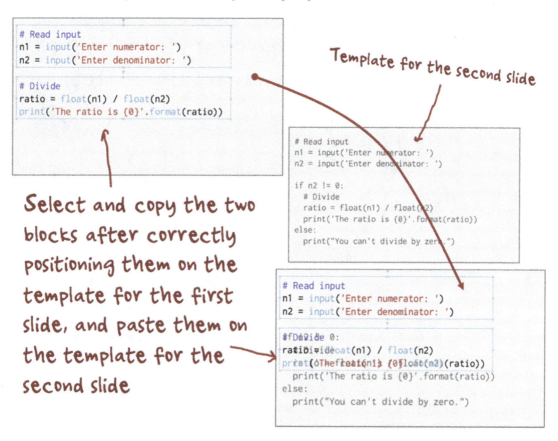

Figure 7-7. *Preparing the switch from the first to the second slide*

For the first block of text, first and second slides coincide because it doesn't move. Figure 7-8 shows how to make the block that moves evolve between the first and the second version of the program: select the second block of text, and use a linear motion to bring it into its correct final position. Adjust the zooming factor of the slide view, and zoom to the highest possible value that lets you see both original and final positions on your screen.

After experiments with various letters, I found that for me, positioning the cross that indicates where the motion starts over an "o" works best for precise positioning. You can position the cross right in the middle of the "o," then bring it right in the middle of where the "o" will ultimately be. If there is no "o" in your text (or in your shape text), you can always add one both to the block to move and to the gray template, then remove the letter when the motion path is correctly set – it's just editable text, after all.

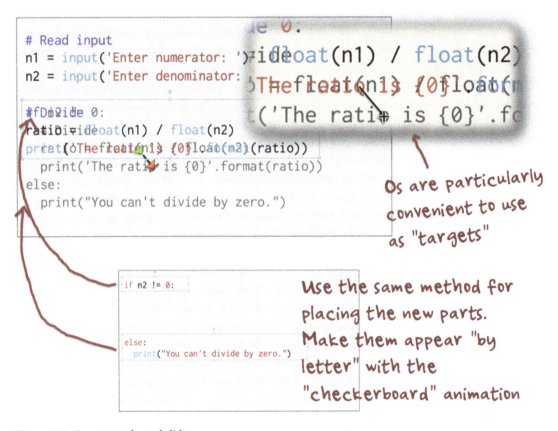

Figure 7-8. *Journey to the end slide*

The only remaining task is to make the new text appear. Using the same technique, position blocks of text over the template, and animate them with a "checkerboard" appearance with (very important) the "by letter" animation selected. Select the gray templates and delete them, unset any Smooth Start/Smooth End with motions, delete any useless leftover slide, and you are ready to show very smoothly to your audience how to switch from a naive version of the code, to a slightly less naive version of it. At which point it could be useful to point out that zero is not the only value against which we have to protect our program: the keyboard might be in caps-lock mode, users might hit a letter by mistake; anything can happen and it would be nice to have a mechanism to catch any type of input error, even unexpected ones. There is one, but I'm supposed to talk about presentation software techniques, and not about programming.

Variations on the techniques I have just exposed are also very useful for presenting topic text that is too large to fit on one slide. If you remember what you have seen in Chapter 5, I had mentioned using a "push from bottom" transition so that the audience gets the feeling that we are panning over a single piece of code. Once again, "push" is what I use when I'm really, really short on time. "Push," in this particular context, has two main drawbacks:

- I have pointed out that unless you are ready to see a large gap moving from bottom to top across the screen during the transition, the bottom margin on the first slide and the top margin on the second slide should both be extremely narrow. That means that your text should extend to the very bottom of the first slide, where it may not be perfectly visible for everybody in the room: I have given classes in computer labs, the screen was extending down almost to the level of desks, and the people in the last rows had many computer screens in their line of sight. It was better to keep empty the very bottom of the slide.

- The second slide completely replaces the first one; it would be nice to repeat the bottom lines of the first slide at the top of the second one as a kind of context reminder and a visual anchor.

To avoid these drawbacks, I use animations, faded transitions, and a fugitive slide. I have illustrated in Figure 7-9 an example I have used in class, a small program in the C language that asks for text, and displays it in reverse. I have created a gray template (copying the text and changing the font color) for each one of the two slides that are needed to display the program in full; I'll refer to the template for the first slide as "first template," and to the template for the second slide as "second template." Each number in Figure 7-9 corresponds to a block of code that I display on a distinct click before commenting it. The main point to notice in Figure 7-9 is that I have repeated the instruction circled in orange on both slides, although this instruction only appears once in the real program. This instruction basically says to the computer to pause the program until the user has entered some text, and it will become my visual anchor that will link the two slides. I have used this specific instruction on purpose: everything that precedes it is mostly some setup, and it's only when the user enters some data that action really starts.

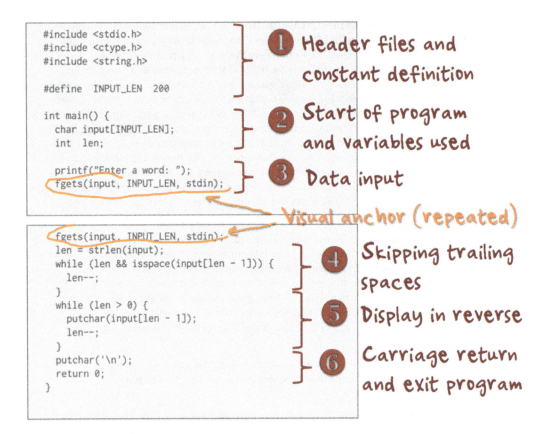

```
#include <stdio.h>
#include <ctype.h>
#include <string.h>

#define  INPUT_LEN  200

int main() {
  char input[INPUT_LEN];
  int  len;

  printf("Enter a word: ");
  fgets(input, INPUT_LEN, stdin);
```

① Header files and constant definition

② Start of program and variables used

③ Data input

Visual anchor (repeated)

```
  fgets(input, INPUT_LEN, stdin);
  len = strlen(input);
  while (len && isspace(input[len - 1])) {
    len--;
  }
  while (len > 0) {
    putchar(input[len - 1]);
    len--;
  }
  putchar('\n');
  return 0;
}
```

④ Skipping trailing spaces

⑤ Display in reverse

⑥ Carriage return and exit program

Figure 7-9. *Planning the slides*

At this point I almost have a storyboard for my example, which begins to look like a Hollywood story: exposition in the first slide, a triggering event (reading some input), and a chain of events before a climax and a conclusion. I'm not sure that printing out a carriage return can really be qualified as the climax, but I can pretend.

I'm going to duplicate both templates; I'll need all these templates firstly for preparing the slides showing each block separately, secondly for the fugitive slide.

First operation, I paste on one copy of the first and of the second templates each block that has to appear separately as a distinct block of text. This block will be colored as in the previous example in a way that is reminiscent of how syntax-colored editors used by programmers would display the text. Figure 7-10 shows how I prepare my first slide, copying each block separately over the gray first template, dragging each block roughly in place as in the figure, before zooming over text and placing every block very precisely with the numerical position values that can be set by right-clicking on each block of text. Blocks will all be animated in the same way ("fade" or "checkerboard" appearance animated by letter, a "fade" or even a simple "appear" for everything at once are all possible options). As I don't want to show an empty slide, the first animation starts "With Previous," immediately when the slide is shown.

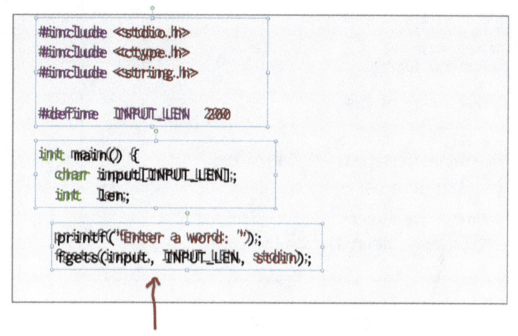

Figure 7-10. *Animating the first part of the code*

I must also use a second copy of the first template to prepare a fugitive slide that will link the two slides together. However, on this fugitive slide I'm going to have two different blocks of text: what will no longer appear on the second slide, and what will still be on the second slide, which I call the "visual anchor." Figure 7-11 illustrates this phase, with the "visual anchor" being the line that starts with fgets. I'm placing the two blocks exactly like I've done earlier.

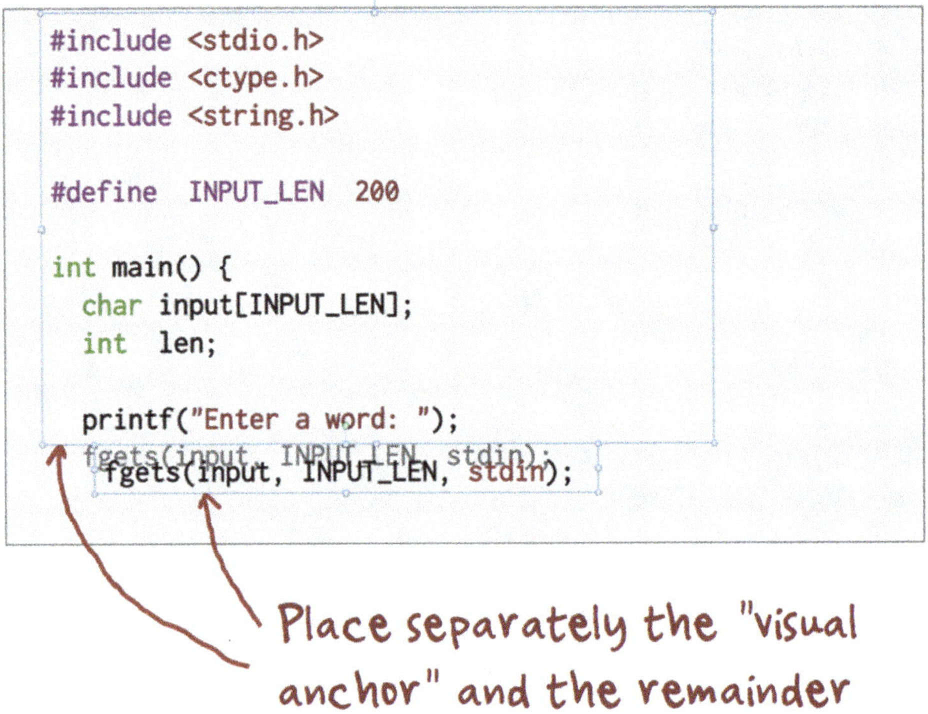

```c
#include <stdio.h>
#include <ctype.h>
#include <string.h>

#define  INPUT_LEN  200

int main() {
  char input[INPUT_LEN];
  int  len;

  printf("Enter a word: ");
  fgets(input, INPUT_LEN, stdin);
  fgets(input, INPUT_LEN, stdin);
```

Place separately the "visual anchor" and the remainder

Figure 7-11. *Preparing the fugitive slide*

Animating the fugitive slide is a bit more interesting than animating the other slides. Using the editing options, I "cut" my visual anchor and "paste" it onto the *second* template. The block of text will be at exactly the same position as it was on the first template because of the position-keeping feature that I have mentioned earlier in this chapter. Figure 7-12 shows what I do next. I have told you earlier that o's are excellent targets for motions, and when there is no **o** in the text to move, nothing prevents from adding one; this is precisely what I have done in Figure 7-12, replacing *fgets* with *fgetos* both in the pasted block and in the template simply to have an **o** in the block I want to move. Then I can define precisely the motion path before removing the additional letter.

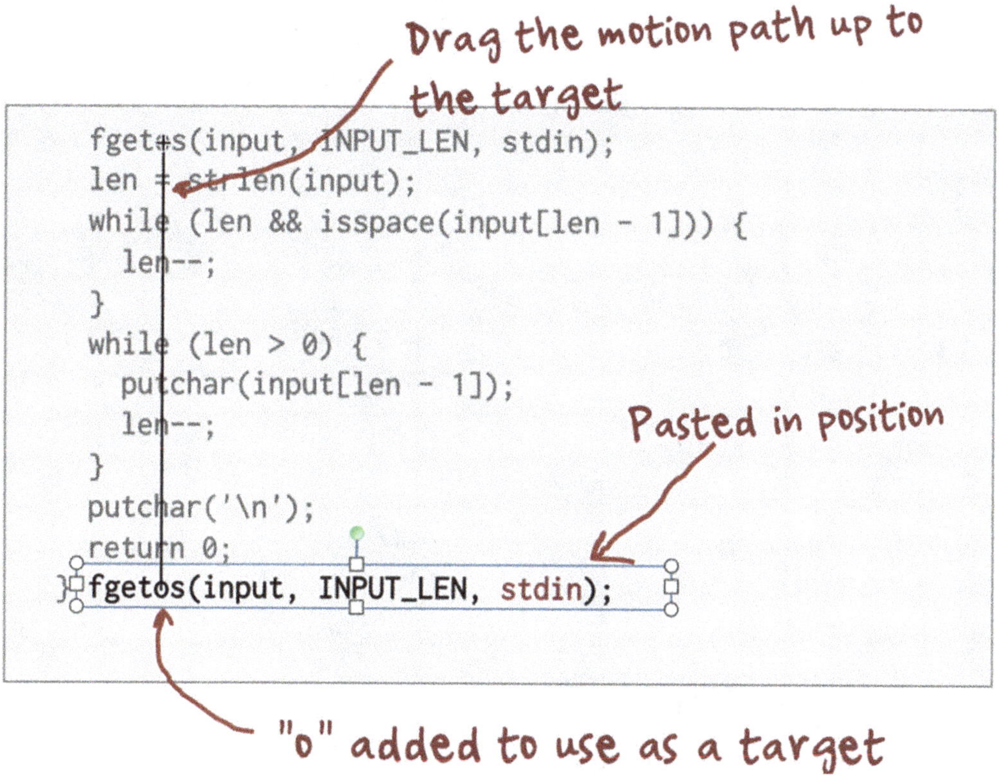

Drag the motion path up to the target

```
fgets(input, INPUT_LEN, stdin);
len = strlen(input);
while (len && isspace(input[len - 1])) {
    len--;
}
while (len > 0) {
    putchar(input[len - 1]);
    len--;
}
putchar('\n');
return 0;
fgetos(input, INPUT_LEN, stdin);
```

Pasted in position

"o" added to use as a target

Figure 7-12. *Preparing animation in the fugitive slide*

This motion of my visual anchor is the only move that needs precision. Figure 7-13 illustrates the next steps required: in step 1, I'm removing, if I haven't already done it, my visual anchor from over my first template. Then I'm copying the anchor, with the motion added, from the second template where I have defined the motion, back into the first template. Before doing anything else, I double-check that Smooth Start and Smooth End are disabled.

My visual anchor is now ready to move, on the fugitive slide, from its position on the first slide to its position on the second slide. I still have to take care of the lines of code on the first slide that will not seen on the second slide. To make them vanish, I'm going to make them move up at exactly the same speed as the anchor, and make them fade out at the same time for good measure. In Figure 7-12 I have shown how to add motion to the visual anchor, and that was relatively easy because I had a starting point and an ending point. For the code that vanishes, we have no ending point; the problem is that if I want exactly the same speed for both blocks, the duration of the move must be identical, **and** the distance traveled must be identical. Without an ending point to use as a target, it's impossible to set precisely the distance. To make sure I have the same movement as for the anchor, in set 3 of Figure 7-13 I simply copy and paste the anchor elsewhere on the slide; the idea is that I'm going to keep, as a kind of wrapper, the box with the motion associated, but replace the text. This is what I have done in step 4 of Figure 7-13: after highlighting the text that I want to move (and when I say the text, I really mean the text, not the text box), I copied it into the text box that was already set with the correct motion.

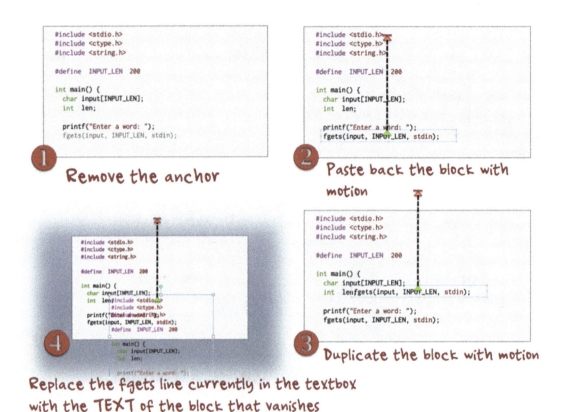

Figure 7-13. *Animating the fugitive slide*

The last operations, shown in Figure 7-14, are straightforward: I have removed the original block of text corresponding to what must disappear, I have widened (as the original text was wider than the visual anchor) the new moving block of text and placed it as usual over the template. Then I have added a faded disappearance effect, set all durations to the same value (two seconds), and set all start time to "With Previous" so that everything gets underway as soon as I switch to this slide. Finally, as this is a fugitive slide, in the transition pane I have set an automated transition to the next slide immediately when animations have finished. I'll then make the second transition appear with a faded transition (in case the motion of the visual anchor is wrong by one pixel), and I'll immediately display the first block after the anchor on the second slide.

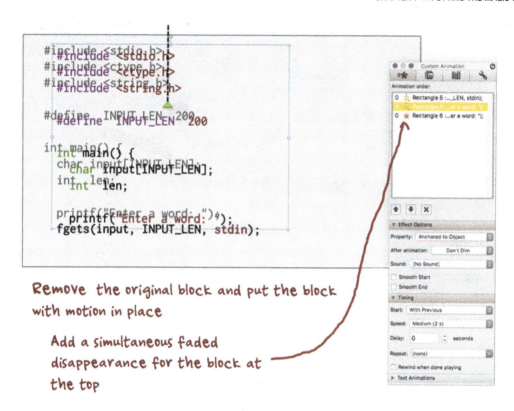

Remove the original block and put the block with motion in place

Add a simultaneous faded disappearance for the block at the top

Figure 7-14. *Fugitive slide, final state*

Figure 7-15 shows the whole sequence when the slides are shown. The three images at the top show, click after click, the first slide; the three images at the bottom show, click after click, the second slide, and you see in the middle a transient image of the fugitive slide, with the red arrow indicating movement. Of course, "first slide" and "second slide" are implementation choices: each image could as well be a different slide if you decide to make a heavier use of transitions rather than animations. I have added on all slides (including the fugitive one) reverse.c, which is the name of the program and remains at the same place from the beginning of the sequence to its end. As all the moves are carried out through animations and idempotent transitions, I can keep elements at the same place (I usually also keep boxes representing variables - memory storage – and the values stored there at any given moment).

I'd like to bring your attention on a point that is more important for the presenter than for the audience: clicks. I have already said in Chapter 5 that it's important that a visual change follows a click as quickly as possible; if there is a delay, you may think you didn't press the button on your remote control firmly enough and do it again, thus skipping a beat by accident.

141

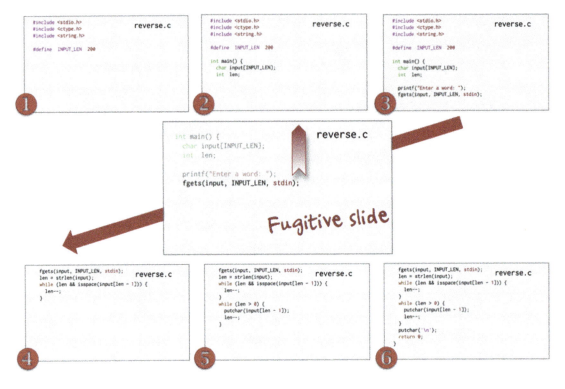

Figure 7-15. *Presenting code spanning "two slides" (… plus a fugitive one)*

I can add other disturbing cases for a presenter, such as slides that *should* be fugitive but aren't and require an additional click to switch to the next slide. As a presenter, you have something on your screen, you click, and a slide may have replaced another slide but nothing changes (or hardly anything changes) on screen: an unsettling situation, which you'd rather avoid.

■ **First Rule of Clicks**   Every click brings a visible change onscreen.

There are other points to consider. In Figure 7-15, I probably had another slide before step 1. If I animate what is shown in step 1 (and I should do it for consistency if I animate any other block of text), animation should be started "With Previous," in other words, automatically when the slide is shown, and not on a click. Suppose I have *not* added the name of the program; I would have a completely empty slide shown until I click. When you are presenting, you aren't glancing at your screen or at your monitor all the time; you are also supposed to establish eye contact with your audience. You don't want to display an empty slide for a few seconds, until you notice that something is wrong.

■ **Second Rule of Clicks**   A click never takes you to an empty slide, unless something appears automatically and immediately.

Finally, I must also take care of clicks in step 4 of Figure 7-15, just after the fugitive slide. Let's review what happens when I click after step 3: all the code moves up at the same speed, the visual anchor reaches its place for the second slide, while the remainder fades away while moving up. The slide on which these animations are defined is a fugitive slide; it switches automatically to the next one on which I'll have the visual anchor at the top (of course, it requires no animation at this stage). My presentation follows so far what I have called the First and Second Rules of Clicks. What about the block of text that follows the visual anchor and is an object unseen so far: should it appear automatically, or on click? My opinion is that it should appear automatically. There is no reason to pause after the fugitive slide; if you do, it looks like you are begging for a murmur of admiration for this awesome and cool animation. The animation isn't here to look awesome and cool, the animation is here to maintain continuity; if you pause, you introduce a break and ruin everything. In fact, the real reason for this animation is that slides aren't high enough. I told you in Chapter 1 that for presenting code I prefer using a 4:3 size. In Figure 7-15 the code is shown on slides in a 16:9 format, on which I can display fewer lines. Suppose just for a moment that I use slides in the 4:3 format: the moment when I need to switch would be postponed, and the click at the end of step 3 could trigger the appearance of the block of text shown in step 4, and nothing more. I believe that a fugitive slide should be transparent, and never interfere with my "story," which is the code I'm showing. Therefore the purpose of the click at the end of step 3 truly is to display the text in step 4, which should start automatically; the fugitive slide is anecdotal.

■ **Third Rule of Clicks**   The real purpose of a click that triggers a fugitive slide is to animate what immediately follows the fugitive slide.

The Vanishing Slides

When I discussed in Chapter 6 the reasons for animating a presentation, I mentioned displaying text and graphics as you are talking, showing a movement that belongs to the story, and finally staging sequences. The motion in the preceding example belongs to staging; however, it has a functional reason: gluing together pieces of code that cannot be displayed on one slide, with more flexibility than what a "push" or "pan" transition would allow. My final example will be pure staging; we are going to review a number of possible options, on a scale ranging from the most basic use of PowerPoint to a sequence where the audience is unable to say when we are switching from one slide to the next or what is on each slide. As I'm talking about "staging," my example, for once, won't be technical but linked to the history of theater: I'll present a few traditional characters from the Italian *Commedia dell'arte*, a popular, mostly improvised theater form featuring, as Chinese opera, masked actors. It appeared in Italy in the 16th century and later had a strong influence on European comedy; you even find very recognizable echoes of *Commedia dell'arte* in some of Mozart's operas.

Figure 7-16 shows what someone unfamiliar with PowerPoint or with presentations might produce: following scrupulously the "instructions" displayed by presentation software, I have one slide with a title and five bullet points (which is what you find as the maximum recommended when you search on the Web for "how many bullet points should I have on a slide"...). The descriptions of five classic stock characters have been compiled from various sources. I would advise you to record your reading aloud everything but the title from this slide, then to download the sample slides for this chapter from the publisher's website, and to click along while you replay your recording: it will be a very good way to experience what the audience would watch and hear.

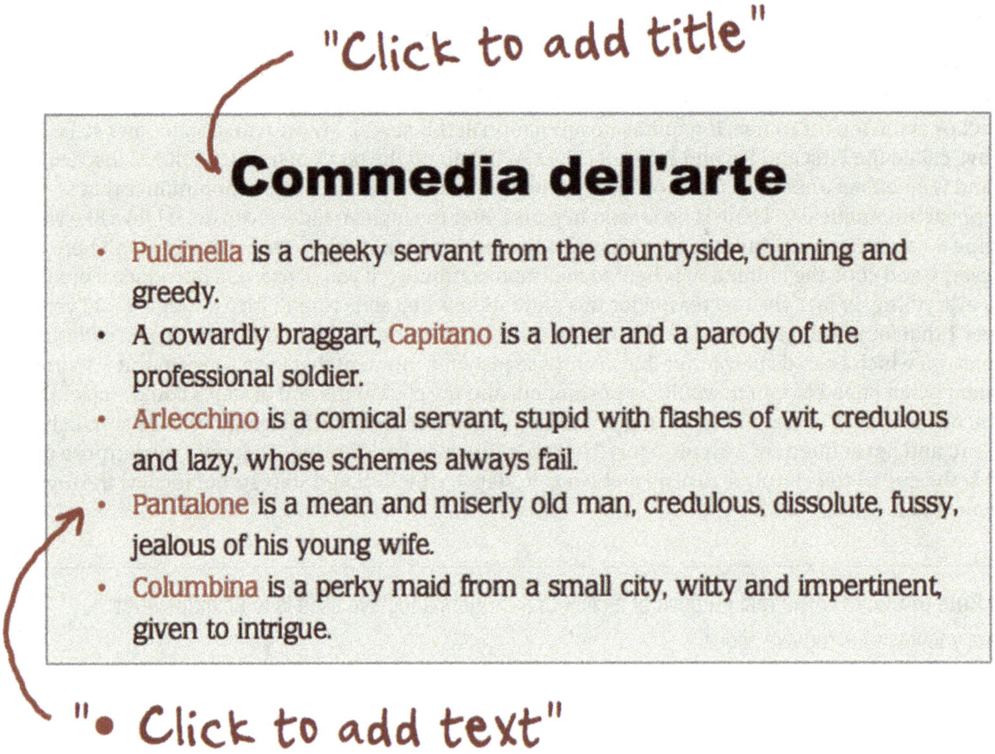

"Click to add title"

Commedia dell'arte

- Pulcinella is a cheeky servant from the countryside, cunning and greedy.
- A cowardly braggart, Capitano is a loner and a parody of the professional soldier.
- Arlecchino is a comical servant, stupid with flashes of wit, credulous and lazy, whose schemes always fail.
- Pantalone is a mean and miserly old man, credulous, dissolute, fussy, jealous of his young wife.
- Columbina is a perky maid from a small city, witty and impertinent, given to intrigue.

"• Click to add text"

Figure 7-16. *A kind of slide seen far too many times*

The obvious flaw of the slide in Figure 7-16 is that there is far too much text on it; in fact, there is probably almost everything that a presenter would want to say in an introduction to these characters, except perhaps a description of traditional costumes. The presenter who masters the subject might talk a bit more, but there may be time constraints. A presenter who feels a little less at ease would read the slide, or paraphrase it, which rarely tricks the audience into the feeling that the presenter adds value to the slides.

I have shown in Figure 7-17 what will usually be the next step: sites that advise four or five bullet points per slide also advise five words per bullet point; another "rule" (probably born out of serious empirical studies and scientific evidence) says "a maximum of 33 words per slide." Armed with these solid rules, I have summarized each character in as few words as I could, bringing my total number of words (including the title) down to 21. What the presenter will say will still be what was shown in Figure 7-16; however, for the audience the presenter will no longer be reading his or her slides and there will be a feeling of added value. I have also in the process gotten rid of bullet points, which add nothing. To avoid dumping the description of all characters at once, you can add animation, making everything appear (plain appear or fade) by paragraph, so that one name appears each time you click. Additionally, you can select the option "dim after animation" that changes the font color of the last line to a far less visible hue each time a new line appears, thus putting the focus on one and only one line.

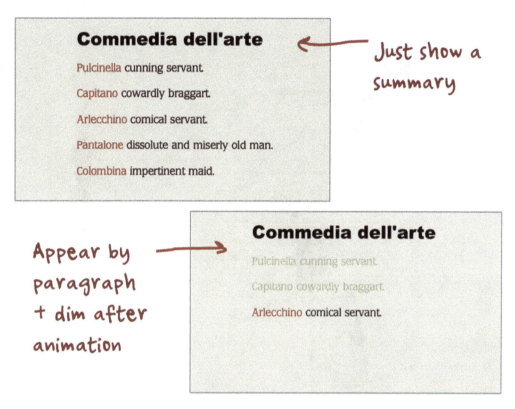

Figure 7-17. *Levels 2 and 3 of PowerPoint mastery*

Don't forget, if you dim paragraphs after animation, to unset the effect for the last line. Otherwise the last click on the slide will change its color, and you will see everything dimmed when you would expect to switch to the next slide.

Now, if all you show in a presentation is text, especially when talking about performing arts, your presentation will indeed be a very sad presentation. The characters of the *Commedia dell'arte* are stock characters, with codified masks and costumes that made them instantly recognizable to a popular audience that was probably partly illiterate; it would be a pity not to show the characters, especially when the famous 19th-century drawings by Maurice Sand are in the public domain (you find them in almost every souvenir shop in Venice or Bergamo, the city of Arlecchino – and of course everywhere on the Web). As you have seen in Chapter 4, if you want to show characters in full (which excludes edge-to-edge images, as these famous illustrations are all vertically oriented) you need to remove the background, which is better done with a tool such as Gimp rather than with the PowerPoint tool; the PowerPoint tool chokes on white ruffs on a light background.

Other changes are required though: if you want to show name and image simultaneously, you can no longer use a single block of text animated by a paragraph as in Figure 7-17. The simplest way to achieve a smooth presentation is probably what is shown in Figure 7-18: not using any animation, but having one slide per character with, for instance, faded transitions. Additionally, I alternate the position of images, one on the right, and then one on the left. I should add that the order of names isn't quite random either, and I alternate one servant (servants are usually the heroes, for all their flaws), and one pompous and ridiculous character. In that way, I always have the "bad guys" on one side, and the "good guys" on the other side, which may help with memorization.

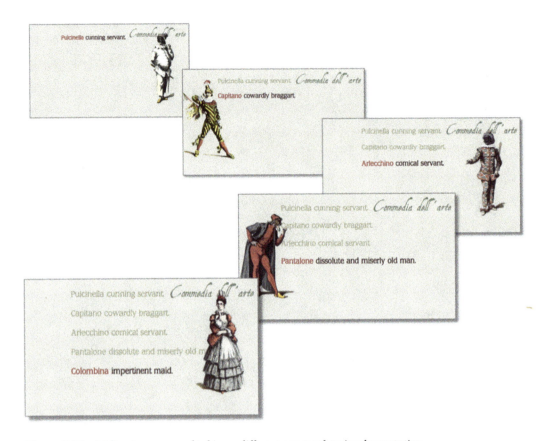

Figure 7-18. *Adding images – and taking a different approach to implementation*

I have kept in Figure 7-18 the names and short descriptions of all characters shown previously, as I had in Figure 7-17. As I have just hinted, the costumes of characters are extremely important for recognition of the various types; do we want the audience to remember names, or costumes and masks? This is a legitimate question to ask and rather than keeping on screen the names of the previous characters, I'd may want to keep a smaller desaturated image rather than dimmed text. This is what I have done in Figure 7-19, neatly aligning the images of characters already introduced on what the combination of scale (smaller images, obtained using a standard 50% reduction of both dimensions) and desaturation gives the illusion of being a line in the background (a technique learned from Bruce Block's *The Visual Story*). If the example given in Figure 7-18 is a good PowerPoint presentation, it still looks like PowerPoint. In Figure 7-19, we are beginning to drift, taking advantage of the slide format to have a more horizontal layout and a screen that ultimately looks far more like a stage – rather appropriate for the topic.

However, if individual slides look rather good, it no longer works so well when you display them in sequence. If we want to maintain continuity throughout the sequence, we should use an idempotent transition because we have some elements that remain in the same place from slide to slide: the *Commedia dell'arte* title, and the already introduced characters, who accumulate slide after slide. With an idempotent transition, the only objects that will move will be the ones that aren't at the same place on two successive slides, and here the huge differences become an issue (in Figure 7-19, a big Arlecchino in the foreground turns into a small Arlecchino in the background). No transition or "cut" introduces unpleasant jumps, and the audience sees too much the switches between slides. Faded transitions aren't that bad, but nevertheless linking the bigger image of Arlecchino on the first slide to the smaller image on the second slide is a connection that the brain won't establish naturally. The audience can understand it, but will have to think hard about it, meanwhile forgetting about Pantalone who should be the focus of attention. There is less text and more images than in Figure 7-18, and yet, as there are more displacements, following the sequence is in the end more demanding. I have nothing against making an audience think, quite the contrary; but I want to make the audience think about what is worth it, and not mentally try to bridge gaps in a presentation that isn't smooth enough. In the end, brain power would be wasted at the wrong place and the message wouldn't be received as intended.

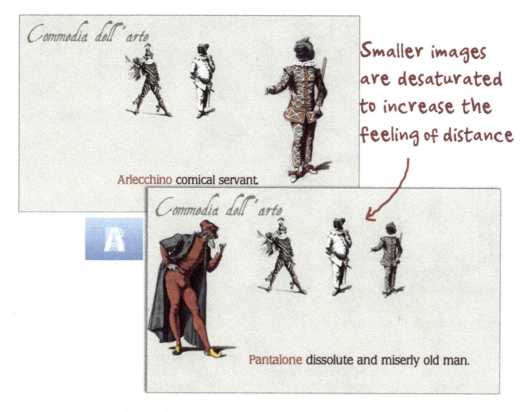

Figure 7-19. *Going almost fully visual*

Additionally, there is something wrong with a faded transition (and that point is true both for Figures 7-18 and -19): on a stage, actors usually don't appear out of nowhere. They come on stage; this is a case where, contrary to the sets of animals, there should be no latency. There is little point making the presentation more theater-like if this effort is at the same time contradicted every time one clicks to show the next slide.

I have in Figure 7-20 reworked the presentation from Figure 7-19 to correct the various issues I have mentioned, by using animation as well as fugitive slides. All transitions are still faded transitions, but animations explicitly show how every image moves from place to place, thus removing the burden of filling the gaps for the audience. Using a technique very similar to the "slanted zoom" I used in Chapter 6 to focus on the lasso in the Gimp toolbox, I combined emphasis (Grow/Shrink again, but this time to shrink) and motion to make every character move to the back. This combined animation takes place at exactly the same moment when the next character comes on stage, "flying in" from, presumably, the wings, either on the left or on the right. A third object is animated at the same time: the short descriptive text, which I have chosen to display using "fade" animated by letter.

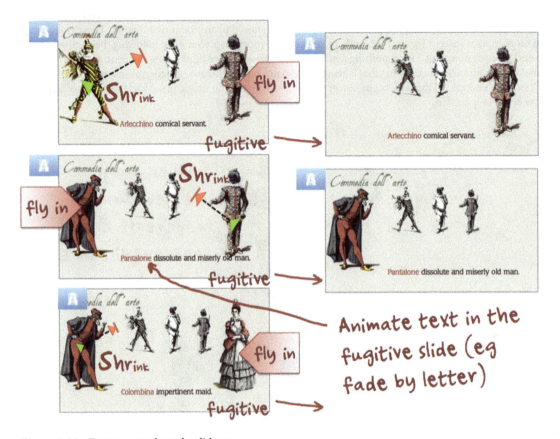

Figure 7-20. *Try to guess where the slides are*

The slide on which all of this takes place is a fugitive slide, for a technical reason: as I mentioned previously, I desaturate the smaller images to accentuate the illusion (on a flat surface) of aligning them in the background. There is, among emphasis effects, an animation called "desaturate"; however, at least in my version of PowerPoint it turns a color image to gray. I want images to be only partly desaturated: colors are grayer, fainted, but still there even if it's not completely obvious in Figure 7-20 because of size. As a result, just after I have shrunk the image of a character, I automatically fade into a slide where the smaller image is desaturated.

The most difficult part in all the animation is to place smaller images exactly where the combination of shrinkage and motion takes the bigger images; as all characters move to a slightly different place, you cannot simply copy and paste, and each image requires adjustment by trial and error. It's not as bad as it looks though (I know, I've done it) for five characters.

The result gives you something that looks very much like characters coming on stage one after the other to introduce themselves before sidelining; nobody will be able to tell where slides start and end, most people won't associate your presentation with "slides." They'll probably follow it with far more attention than the bullet-point example in Figure 7-16 and, even if I have no hard evidence to support this assertion, my guess is that a few days later they will remember far more.

Summary

- More cinematic presentations combine simple transitions and simple animations.

- Substituting shapes with an image obtained by a screenshot opens many possibilities.

- Animations and fugitive slides are a more demanding but more effective way than "push" or "pan" to present text that cannot fit on one screen. In particular, it allows you to keep decently sized top and bottom margins, and it also allows you to keep an anchor from the preceding slide into the current one to better link them together.

- Rules of clicks: every click brings a visible change on screen, a click never takes you to an empty slide, and the purpose of a click that triggers a fugitive slide is to animate what immediately follows the fugitive slide.

- Options for presenting one topic are only limited by your imagination. You can switch between techniques (animation versus transition), you can combine them – and in the end you reach a stage where your audience no longer has the feeling of watching slides.

Conclusion

I have tried in this book to explain both the principles that guide me, the techniques I use, and what makes me choose one technique preferably to another one. Although most writers on presentation advise against animation, an advice that makes sense in many business presentations, I strongly believe that whenever you would energetically move your arm in front of a paperboard or grab a marker and start drawing arrows, it means that to present the same topic with PowerPoint you ought to use some kind of animation. I feel a particular urge for animation in many technical presentations, although presentations need not be technical – the *Commedia dell'arte* example proves it – to be enhanced by it. The point, though, is that animation should **never** be gratuitous; it should be considered an implicit component of explanation, even if in some cases the "explanation" is nothing more challenging that linking slides on the screen and sparing your audience the distracting effort of trying to understand how you went from A to B. Sophisticated slide animation is usually achieved using the simplest of means, fades, linear motions, and not by bringing up elements on stage with an Axel jump followed by a backflip.

I raised the question at the end of Chapter 4, where I discussed about image editing, of how far you should go and how much time you should spend on image processing. This question obviously extends to a whole presentation; some operations are relatively time consuming, especially the precise placement of objects on separate slides. You may legitimately consider that some simpler options are "good enough"; I personally don't consider time spent perfecting a presentation as wasted if this presentation is strategically important or will be repeated.

I often quote, when talking about databases, the famous verses by T. S. Eliot:

Where is the wisdom we have lost in knowledge?
Where is the knowledge we have lost in information?

(to which I add *Where is the information we have lost in data?*)

Information, these days, is merely one click away. As an instructor (in the widest acceptance), dumping information isn't good enough, because information has become a commodity; it's only by sharing your vision that you help your audience turn information into knowledge. Presentation software is certainly not the only way to do it, but in spite of its ubiquity, it's curiously underrated as a means to effectively transmit knowledge, as opposed to putting an audience to sleep. I must say that the often terribly boring slides supplied by textbook publishers don't do much to restore the image of presentation software. Break free from the default template, from the "Click here to add" routine, and you'll discover that the limiting factor isn't so much the medium as it is imagination.

APPENDIX A

■ ■ ■

Introducing Oneself

Who in the world am I? Ah, THAT's the great puzzle.

—Lewis Carroll (1832-1898)

Unless you are a living legend or were introduced by somebody else, introducing oneself is usually the purpose of the first slides in a presentation. It's not only a matter of courtesy, but also a way to present your credentials and your qualifications for speaking. It happens, sometimes, that you are talking on a topic because nobody else wanted to do it, but these are circumstances that are better ignored. When I say "oneself" I'm not necessarily talking about your physical self; "oneself" may be the company in the name of which you are presenting. In that case, the purely personal aspect of an introduction may be limited to the title on your business card. The almost mandatory exercise of introduction, though, is also a great way to teach your audience the visual codes that you are using, and it's mostly from this standpoint that I'll discuss introduction in this appendix.

Teaching Your Rules

Let's say that the presentation is about hamburger flipping. A typical "About Me" slide will look like Figure A-1. Most people modestly keep to one slide when talking about themselves (you sometimes see two or more slides when they talk about their company). Remember, once again, that the number of slides is irrelevant; it's the time spent that counts. You shouldn't hesitate to use many slides if they enliven that (usually, let's admit it, rather boring) part of your talk.

© Stéphane Faroult 2016
S. Faroult, *Getting the Message Across*, DOI 10.1007/978-1-4842-2295-9_8

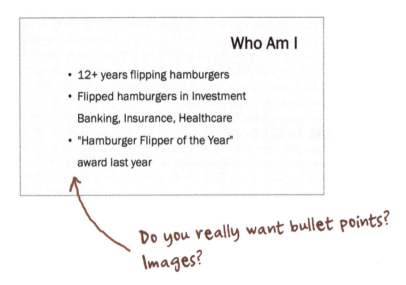

Figure A-1. *A typical "About Me" slide. You can do better*

If you aren't using bullet points in your presentation, you shouldn't be using any in your introduction. If you are using images in your presentation, you should use images in your introduction. If you are using special transitions between parts, of which I gave a few examples in Chapter 5, one such transition before the introduction and another one for ending it will drill your codes once and for all. If you plan to use in your presentation such effects as a background color switch or an aside (both introduced in Chapter 2), they are usually easy to bring into an introduction – books you have written if you are an author, or social media accounts if most of your writing is online are, for instance, natural asides. If you have given a general theme to your presentation, use it in your introduction as well.

Don't use in your introduction any effect that will never be seen again in the course of your presentation, but teach your audience your rules so that the next time an effect appears it's correctly interpreted without any effort. Knowing the rules will keep your audience focused on your message.

Time and History

You usually want to stress a long experience of what you are talking of; if your company has been around for a long time, you also want to tell it, because most companies collapse in their first years and longevity inspires confidence for a future business relationship. An alternative to stating a number of years of relevant experience, and a good way to involve your audience from the beginning, is to start with a riddle. I often show, whenever I'm talking about the SQL database language, a collection of small pictures of the world leaders when I first learned this language: Ronald Reagan, Yuri Andropov (unlikely to be recognized), Margaret Thatcher, Indira Gandhi, and Deng Xiaoping - add any local head of state that fits the place where you are talking. I only show the year on the next slide, as huge digits occupying the full surface of the slide. Alternatively, you can take your inspiration from these birthday cards listing the notable events from a given year; you can also, if a very famous local landmark was built shortly after the year you want to stress, find and show a picture of the place that year. In all cases, show the pictures first, and the year only later, to give your audience a chance to try to guess.

If you cannot boast of several decades in business, you can make whatever you can claim more respectable with a humorous twist. Pick any young celebrity who has only very recently come into the limelight, and try to find a picture of them the right number of years ago; the result should look far more impressive than it really is. I also played once for a friend the card "it seems so long ago already" by flipping back (correct) year numbers over (wrong) pictures that exaggerated the amount of time that passed. Each successive year (there were five of them) was one less than the previous one, but pictures were moving back by ten years each time.

References

Besides years of experience, prestigious employers or customers can also boost your credibility. Rather than a boring list, you can get some inspiration from the Commedia dell'arte example of Chapter 7, replacing the images of characters with company logos. When companies aren't household names, it's probably better to focus on industries or business sectors. Industries are also better illustrated by photographs, either one per slide, edge to edge, or several small pictures appearing one by one.

The mandatory exercise of introduction should really be seen as an opportunity for preparing your audience to your presentation style, and at the same time to set a standard for yourself.

APPENDIX B

■ ■ ■

Licensing Issues

Durch Geschenke erwirbt man keine Rechte.
A gift confers no rights.

—Friedrich Nietzsche (1844-1900)

I have no legal qualification, but I'd like in this appendix to point out a number of issues I have already hinted in this book: you cannot use *any* image or *any* font in your presentations. In fact, it's an ethical as much as a legal issue. You shouldn't deprive anybody from a fair reward for their efforts; you should also have the honesty to acknowledge what you borrow, even when there is no financial implication. Often, practice is more complicated than theory; some ideas you honestly think are original are sometimes unconscious reminiscences; authorship may be poorly known – just consider quotes, which are very often misattributed. The history of art, whether it's in sculpture, painting, or literature, is full of borrowings, including by the biggest names.

A recent intellectual creation belongs to its creator, or sometimes to another entity to which the author transferred the rights by contract (such as publishers for books). Unless you have a special contract, or the rightsholder decided to waive some of them, you cannot copy what belongs to others who hold the "copyright." After a number of years that depends on the country, creations are deemed to belong to the "public domain," where authors can also put them from the start. However, even "public domain" is a notion that demands qualification; I remember seeing at the entrance of an archaeology museum a sign "you are welcome to take pictures for your personal use," which implies that you cannot necessarily use in any context a photograph that **you** took with **your own** camera of an exhibit a few thousand years old. Museums need money too, and depending on what you want to do with a picture you may have to pay some fees.

Other than the origin of what you want to use, your purpose is also highly important to decide whether you can legitimately incorporate in your presentation a production from someone else: if your aim is to make money, it seems fair to return a modest share of the pie to whomever contributed to your goal. A rightsholder may take a more lenient view if your goal isn't commercial, but it's easy to be generous with the labor of others: the original author, who eats and has bills to pay too, may not agree with your distributing his or her work for free. Licenses define what you can do.

Generally speaking, using material for education is considered fair, although the cost of education makes one wonder where the "commercial" qualification begins and ends, even at non-profit institutions. Let's finally add, in the United States, the doctrine of "fair use" (which sometimes exists elsewhere as "fair dealing") that allows free use of copyrighted material for mere illustration, as well as other purposes such as parody that are less relevant to technical presentations.

As you have understood, licensing issues are a jungle that you should navigate cautiously. Even when my purpose isn't commercial, I try to stick to material that I *could* use for a commercial purpose. Just in case.

© Stéphane Faroult 2016
S. Faroult, *Getting the Message Across*, DOI 10.1007/978-1-4842-2295-9_9

Fonts

The case of fonts is a bit special. First of all, a font is software; it's common (I have done it in this book) to use the word *font* to refer to a characteristic letter shape, but in fact the correct word in that case is *typeface*. A font, strictly speaking, is a piece of software that enables a device to draw the typeface. Typefaces can be copyrighted in most countries (as artistic work), but not in the United States, where only fonts (in practice, files) can be copyrighted as software. Your operating system comes with fonts with which you can create commercial graphics and documents; you may have stronger restrictions (such as "personal use only") with free fonts that you find on the Web. Make sure that the fonts that you are using allow commercial desktop use.

Font licensing soon becomes murky because fonts can be embedded in a slide-deck; if you don't embed them, they will be replaced, if not found, by a hopefully close equivalent on the computer where you are running your presentation. Because letter width or height may be significantly different (I discussed differences between fonts in Chapter 1), font substitution usually breaks alignments and, generally speaking, layouts. If you expect the presentation to run on a different computer from the one it was prepared on, you probably want to embed fonts, but then you are in a case different from "document creation"; embedding fonts mean redistributing software, and therefore you need a more generous license, which allows embedding. Let's also add that, for instance, some versions of PowerPoint allow two different types of embedding: only the glyphs (a general term for letter, digit, punctuation…) that you are using in your text, or the full font. The first case results in smaller files (especially if you are using a special font only for a very short message), but it will prevent any last-minute change, even the correction of a typo, that requires a glyph so far unused.

If a font isn't licensed for embedding, restrictions are recorded inside it, and you won't be able to include it with your slides anyway; whether you'll get a warning is a completely different matter, and you may discover, as I have a couple of times, that some fonts are wrong in the course of your presentations. If nothing unduly wraps around, you can take consolation in the fact that your audience doesn't know how the slide should have looked.

Images

Images are probably the main focus of licensing issues. Of course, you can buy rights to images, but in many cases you'll probably want to use free images. Most web engines allow searching for images by license, sometimes referred to as "usage rights"; sometimes the filter is fairly visible on the search page, and sometimes you need to explore advanced options. Thus, Google will give you the choice between the following:

- Labeled for reuse with modification
- Labeled for reuse
- Labeled for noncommercial reuse with modification
- Labeled for noncommercial reuse

Bing suggests the following:

- All Creative Commons
- Public domain
- Free to share and use
- Free to share and use commercially
- Free to modify, share, and use
- Free to modify, share, and use commercially

Yahoo proposes the same filters as Bing, except the first one (a blanket category), and Flickr filters are pretty close as well.

I certainly understand and respect the wishes of a serious photographer who has carefully composed and lighted a picture of not seeing it modified. However, as you have seen in Chapter 4, images often require some editing; something as simple as a mismatch between the format of a photograph and the format of your slides will demand cropping, which is a modification. Additionally, I most often chose to remove the background, which gives me more freedom to recompose images in a way that better suits my discourse. As a consequence, I only search for pictures that are not only free to use commercially, but also free to modify.

Unfortunately, this isn't the end of your troubles. Such a filter will usually return two broad categories of images: Public Domain ones, free to use and for which you don't even need to indicate the name of the author (if known); and Creative Commons images. Creative Commons pictures come themselves in several flavors, some of which explicitly forbid commercial usage or modification and won't be returned; if you search for commercially usable Creative Commons pictures, you'll basically get two types of Creative Commons licenses, CC-BY and CC-BY-SA. CC stands, as you have certainly guessed, for Creative Commons, BY basically means that you must give credit to the author (fair!), and SA stands for *Share Alike*, which is defined as (I'm quoting from the Creative Commons site):

> *If you remix, transform, or build upon the material, you must distribute your contributions under the same license as the original.*

Share Alike confuses me. I understand it if I were to improve a picture (reframing, playing on contrast or colors) and focusing on the picture alone. When the picture becomes just one element lost in 1000 slides or more (which corresponds for me to a one-term course), I don't consider that my having to make my slide-deck CC-BY-SA would be fair if I don't want to. Additionally, the amount of work that goes into my "contribution" may far outweigh the amount of work that went into the original – it takes far more time to remove the background of a candid picture than to point and shoot. This isn't meant, of course, to minimize the original work, but all things considered I prefer shunning CC-BY-SA material in favor of CC-BY material, which is in ample supply.

When publishing free images, the policy at Apress is to use either Public Domain or CC-BY content. In particular, content made available under Creative Commons licenses that have the Share Alike (-SA) suffix cannot be published.

APPENDIX C

Documents

Le secret d'ennuyer est celui de tout dire.
The secret of being boring is to say everything.

—Voltaire (1694-1778)

"Can you send me your slides?" is a phrase that you hear often in a big company after (or sometimes before) you give a presentation – as *slides* have become the mandatory medium of presentations. In my life as a consultant, I have always been most reluctant to leave my slides behind – I have invested time in them, not necessarily in paid hours; additionally, some of my slides may have been recycled from previous presentations, and created during a gig with another customer. The fact that I try to limit text on my slides and that my slide-decks are usually very voluminous – no such thing as including a few images to inflate the size of a .pptx file – are excellent excuses for politely declining such a request. Nevertheless, in most cases you want to leave some document, some kind of "management summary" that ensures that what you said won't be distorted or misinterpreted. You are also expected to provide a document when you give a seminar; a "student manual" when you give professional training; and it's judicious to supply course notes to students, especially when you or some of your students are foreign and oral communication on its own can lead to misunderstandings. Additionally, and it's my personal opinion, I prefer people to listen and watch when I talk rather than take extensive notes.

Document generation is the area where the boring slides of traditional PowerPoint presentations shine in comparison to what is advocated in this book; you save your boring slides as a PDF file and you are done. "Shine" is of course to take with a big pinch of salt, as I have always considered raw slide printouts as rather poor documents. It's however far easier to print ten slides with five bullet points each than one hundred animated slides with little text. When you present many slides and have a cinematic approach, some of your slides are very similar to the preceding one because animation uses transitions and are redundant in a document, and other slides become illegible when printed because of superimposed objects that are supposed to move around or appear on different clicks during the presentation. If you need to provide a companion document, and once again you usually have to, you must prepare a document that is different from your slides. It's in your document that you can have a footer with a copyright notice, not on the slides that you present. I have experimented with a few types of documents, and here are some ideas.

Pure Text Document

For a relatively short presentation, a companion text document works well. Preparing the text document in parallel to the slides may help you both structure your presentation, and rehearse it – having written down what you want to say bolsters your confidence when you have to present slides with little or no text. You can put in your document spreadsheet-generated charts (better replaced by shapes in your presentation as explained in Chapter 3), as well as tables of figures to support your claims, and generally speaking, the

© Stéphane Faroult 2016
S. Faroult, *Getting the Message Across*, DOI 10.1007/978-1-4842-2295-9_10

work documents you used to prepare your slides. Think of the document as a reference document, and of your presentation as a more or less detailed summary. You can also add figures to your document by taking screenshots of some key slides (all the figures in this book are screenshots of slides, in which some images are often screenshots themselves).

Speaker's Notes

I find a pure text document less suitable for a presentation of more than two hours, whether it's a seminar or a course. Alternatively, you can use the document generation facilities of presentation software, in particular, "Speaker's Notes." Instead of starting with writing a document that you later illustrate with slides, you start from your completed slide-deck. Duplicate your slide-deck, select one representative slide per sequence, if necessary modify it to make it suitable for printing, remove all the others, and add a summary of whatever you want to say for the whole sequence to the speaker's notes. In some cases, some slides in the new document may be synthetic slides compounded from several slides shown in the presentation. Always remove from the document break slides and, generally speaking, any slide intended to be an element of surprise; only keep slightly boring slides. Documents in a seminar are usually distributed before the seminar, so that attendees can scribble notes on them, and people who arrive early start browsing the documents while sipping a cup of coffee. Keep some cartridges to maintain attention and incite attendees to watch the screen rather than follow in the document; a seminar is for the speaker a long-distance run.

This exercise allows providing a 50 to 100-page solid companion document for a one-day seminar. As with a pure text document, preparing the notes is an excellent rehearsal and a confidence booster.

Handout Slides for Handout Documents

I have adopted a different strategy with lecture notes (posted in the Learning Management System – LMS - after the lecture). One issue with documents is how thick they should be in relation to the presentation. A complete printout of the slides for a two-day seminar in which you present 800 slides would result, printing 4 slides per page, into a 200-page document. As these documents are usually printed on paper, the result would be far too thick; it may complicate logistics, and nobody really wants to return home after a seminar carrying a big thick document. However, for a series of 1 or 2 1-hour lectures spread over 16 weeks, delivering after each lecture a digital document of 10 to 12 pages (about 50 slides, 4 per page) is more palatable; there is a lesser requirement for a digest.

As when you are using speaker's notes to generate a document, there is nevertheless a need for editing: I usually duplicate my slide-deck, remove slides that are mostly here to punctuate the lecture, and I add comments as blocks of text in a script font (mimicking handwritten notes) to make sure that the key explanations are there, irrespective of the note-taking abilities of students. Figure C-1 shows what some slides of a programming lecture have been turned into in the slide-deck for generating lecture notes.

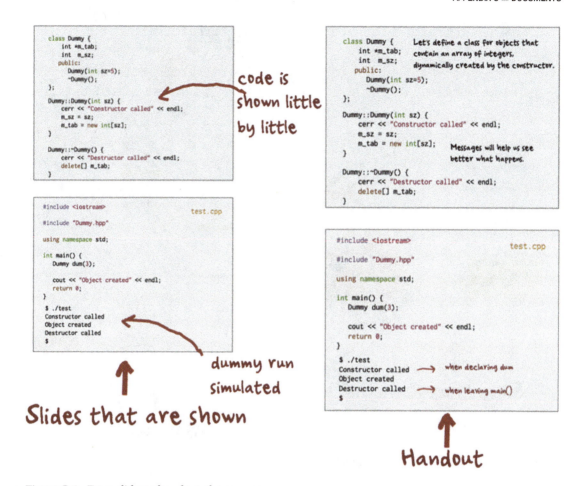

Figure C-1. *From slides to handout, the easy case*

As with speaker's notes-based documents, trouble starts with heavily animated slides, and I have shown in Figure C-2 how I have handed it. On the left-hand side, the slide that was shown was heavily animated – seven clicks, each one of them triggering several simultaneous animations, appearances, disappearances (the screenshot was taken from the "Animation" pane, and each gray square with a number indicates an animation). The purpose of the slide is to step into computer code (the yellow rectangles highlight instructions in turn) to show the crash that can happen (the explosion picture is an allegory) when you fail to specifically define some behaviors. This slide has been copied four times (on the right), which is actually fewer than the different states shown during the lecture, elements removed from each one of the copies so as to get legible slides, and a few words of comments added.

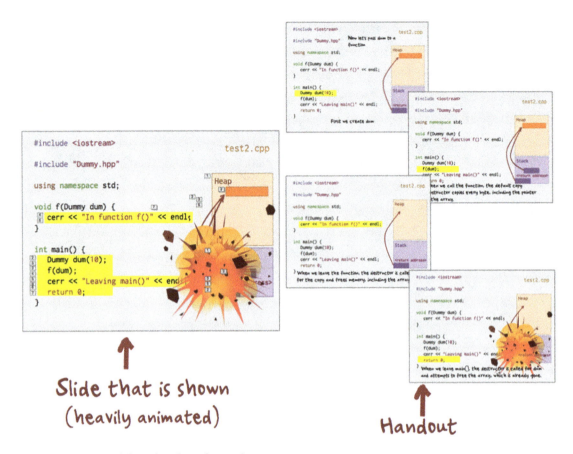

Figure C-2. *From slides to handout, the tougher case*

Sometimes, a motion in the original slide is replaced with an arrow in the corresponding slide of the slide-deck for the handouts. There are also many cases when several slides in the original slide-deck revert to one in the slide-deck for handouts, mostly when you chain slides with idempotent transitions. The ratio of the number of slides in the original presentation to the number of slides in the handout depends mostly on the techniques that you are using to make your presentation lively: transitions mean fewer slides in the handout, animations more slides in the handout. As I combine both methods, I usually end up with slide-decks for handouts that contain just a few less slides than lecture slide-decks. I export the final slide-decks as four-slides-per-page handout PDF files for the consumption of students.

Utilities

Once you have generated your PDF handout files, you may notice two problems:

- If you are using many images the files will be very big.

- If you are creating one handout file per lecture, at the end of the term, when students want to review before the final exam, they may have trouble locating information.

The following describes how I've tried to address these two issues.

Reducing the Size of PDF Files

Having very voluminous slide-decks isn't an issue as long as you don't plan to send them by email or share them; big PDF files intended for distribution are another matter, and, in my versions of PowerPoint at least, I always end up with handout notes PDF files that are as big as the original .pptx files from which they were generated.

I can't remember where I have found on the Web the magical command to massively reduce the size of PDF files, especially when they contain images, but the utility relies on Ghostscript, a well-known free program of which two main versions are available:

- the GNU one, https://www.gnu.org/software/ghostscript/, which only seems to work on Unix-like operating systems;

- and the version maintained by the original developers, https://github.com/ArtifexSoftware/ghostpdl-downloads/releases, for which Windows distributions are also available.

The following script is a bash script (Linux/Mac OSX) that I have written as a wrapper around the suitable Ghostscript command (the line that starts with gs -q) with all the right parameters.

```
if [ $# -eq 0 ]
then
  echo "Usage: $0 pdffile ..." >&2
  exit 1
fi
while [ $# -ne 0 ]
do
    ext=$(basename $1 | cut -f2 -d\. | tr '[:upper:]' '[:lower:]')
    if [ "$ext" != 'pdf' ]
    then
      echo "Skipping $1 (looking for .pdf extension)" >&2
    else
      dname=$(dirname $1)
      bname=$(basename $1 | cut -f1 -d\.)
      if [ $? -eq 0 ]
      then
        oldsize=$(du -k $1 | cut -f1)
        target=${dname}/${bname}_min.pdf
        echo "Compressing $1 to ${target}"
        gs -q -dSAFER -dNOPAUSE -dBATCH -sDEVICE=pdfwrite -dPDFSETTINGS=/ebook \
        -sOUTPUTFILE=${target} -f $1
        newsize=$(du -k $target | cut -f1)
        if [ $newsize -ge $oldsize ]
        then
          echo "$1 not shrunk"
          /bin/rm $target
        else
          echo "$1 ${oldsize}K => ${newsize}K"
        fi
      fi
    fi
  shift
done
```

Indexing Slides

To provide my students with a decent index for lecture notes, I have written (on Mac, porting it to Linux should be easy but I'm not so certain about Windows) a C program that opens and analyzes the content of .pptx files. The source code can be found at https://github.com/sfaroult/slide_index.

If my attempts to try and generate a list of words to index from the text of text boxes and speaker's notes (plus a list of stop words) ended up rather disappointingly, this program works fine when you attach tags (to become index entries) to each slide in your handout slide-deck. The process is illustrated in Figure C-3. I type a semicolon-separated list of tags between square brackets in the speaker's notes area. The program then reads multiple .pptx files, and generates a common index associating with each tag the name of the file where it is found (assumed to be the same name as the .pptx file but with a .pdf extension) and the page where the tag is found. The page number is computed from a parameter that is passed to the program, which is the number of slides per page that will be found in the PDF file. The common index is a Rich Text Format (RTF) file, which can be opened in your favorite text processor. Before saving it as a PDF file, I only change two layout options (which unfortunately cannot be specified in the RTF file):

- I turn the index into a two-column document.

- I set narrow margins.

The result is a quickly generated usable index, which is re-created and updated each time new lecture notes are uploaded to the LMS.

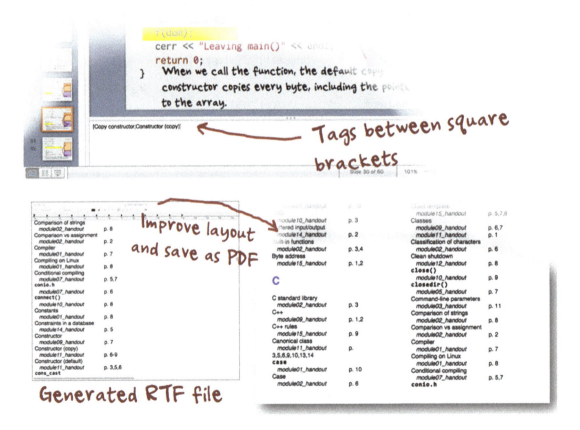

Figure C-3. *Generating an index for multiple PDF handouts*

Index

A

"About Me" slide, 152
Adobe tools, 8
Animate Text, 106
Animations, 161
    appearance/disappearance effects, 106, 108
    audience, 104
    categories, 104
    computer network, 84
    cube transitions, 103
    definition, 103
    "dissolve" pixels, 85
    dynamic slide content, 103
    elephant clipart, 84
    faded transition, 85, 104
    fade works, 106
    grammar, 105
    matching visuals, 104
    network transmission, 84
    peek in, 104–106, 109
    personal technique, 85
    scribbling arrows, 104
    software features, 84
    staging sequences, 104
    successive slides, 85
    wipe *vs.* peek in, 105
Annotations, 25, 39
Ant-sized presenter, 104
Appearance and motion, 119–120
Appearance/disappearance effects, 104, 106, 108
Apress palette, 9
Apress Theme, 15
Automatic extraction, 8

B

Background color, 152
Background removal, 61–63
    color-picker, 74
    "Colors" menu, 74

eraser, 72
    "free select" tool, 74
    geometric shape, 72
    Gimp, 71
    "Image" menu, 70
    light and dark, 72
    line segment, 70
    photograph, 71
    selection, 74
    transparent area, 71, 74
Bar charts, 50
Big picture, 121–123
Binoculars, 37
Blaise Pascal's mechanical calculator, 44
Blink, 114
Bolzano-Weierstrass theorem, 20, 33
Breaking continuity, 25

C

Charts, 40–41
Checkerboard pattern, 108
Cliparts, 41
Color.adobe.com, 8
Color palette, 5
Companion document, 159
Computer code
    animations, 130
    block of text, 134
    checkerboard, 131, 135
    feature, presentation software, 133
    first template, 136–137
    font color, 132
    Format Shape, 133
    fugitiveslide (*see* Fugitive slide)
    instructions, 131
    planning, slides, 135–136
    "push", 135
    splitting, original code, 132
    start and end slides, 130–131
    switching, slides, 133

© Stéphane Faroult 2016
S. Faroult, *Getting the Message Across*, DOI 10.1007/978-1-4842-2295-9

Get the eBook for only $4.99!

Why limit yourself?

Now you can take the weightless companion with you wherever you go and access your content on your PC, phone, tablet, or reader.

Since you've purchased this print book, we are happy to offer you the eBook for just $4.99.

Convenient and fully searchable, the PDF version enables you to easily find and copy code—or perform examples by quickly toggling between instructions and applications.

To learn more, go to http://www.apress.com/us/shop/companion or contact support@apress.com.

GPSR Compliance
The European Union's (EU) General Product Safety Regulation (GPSR) is a set
of rules that requires consumer products to be safe and our obligations to
ensure this.

If you have any concerns about our products, you can contact us on

ProductSafety@springernature.com

In case Publisher is established outside the EU, the EU authorized
representative is:

Springer Nature Customer Service Center GmbH
Europaplatz 3
69115 Heidelberg, Germany

www.ingramcontent.com/pod-product-compliance
Lightning Source LLC
Chambersburg PA
CBHW080414060326
40689CB00019B/4233